WILFRED OWEN
THE COMPLETE POEMS AND FRAGMENTS

Preface.

This book is not about heroes. English Poetry is not yet fit to speak of them.

Nor is it about battles, and glory of battles & lands, nor about any deeds or lands, nor anything about any might, majesty, dominion or power except War.

Above all I am not concerned with Poetry. The subject of it is War, and the pity of War.

The Poetry is in the pity.

Yet these elegies are not in no sense consolatory to this generation. They may be to the next. All a poet can do today is warn. That is why the true War Poet must be truthful.

If I thought the letter of this book would last, I might have used proper names; but if the spirit of it survives Prussia — my ambition and those names will be content; they have achieved themselves fresher fields than Flanders,...

WILFRED OWEN
The complete poems and fragments
edited by JON STALLWORTHY

VOLUME I **The poems**

W. W. Norton and Company

NEW YORK · LONDON

Published in England in 1983 jointly by
Chatto & Windus · The Hogarth Press and Oxford University Press

Published in the United States of America in 1984 by
W. W. Norton & Company, Inc, 500 Fifth Avenue,
New York, NY 10110.

This edition has been published by arrangement with New Directions Publishing Corp.

All rights reserved. No part of this publication may be reproduced, stored in a retrieval system, or transmitted in any form, or by any means, electronic, mechanical, photocopying, recording, or otherwise, without the prior permission of the publisher.

The Poems, Manuscripts and Fragments of Wilfred Owen
© The Executors of Harold Owen's Estate 1963 and 1983

Foreword, Biographical Table, Introduction, List of Abbreviations,
Notes and Appendix C
© Jon Stallworthy 1983

'Two Fusiliers', p. 125, by Robert Graves
© Robert Graves

First American Edition, 1984

ISBN 0-393-01830-X (2-volume set)

Printed in Great Britain

FOREWORD

This edition seeks to establish the texts and the chronology of all surviving poems and fragments by Wilfred Owen, to map their manuscripts, and to offer such factual (as distinct from interpretative) notes as the reader may need to understand them. In this endeavour, it builds upon foundations laid by previous editors – Siegfried Sassoon (assisted by Dame Edith Sitwell), Edmund Blunden, Cecil Day Lewis, and Dr Dominic Hibberd – to the last of whom I owe a particular debt. Dr Hibberd has been at work on a critical study of Owen's poems while I have been editing the texts, and he has been more than generous in sharing his solutions of our common problems.

Editions of this kind necessarily bring together the work and insights of many people, and I should like to record especial gratitude to the editors of the *Collected Letters*, Mr John Bell and the late Harold Owen, Dr Cathrael Kazin who transcribed and dated many of the manuscripts, Miss Catharine Carver the paragon of publishers' editors, Mrs Margaret Babbage, Mr Nicolas Barker, Mrs Edmund Blunden, Mr Peter Croft, Professor S. B. Das, Mr Patric Dickinson, Dr Christopher Dowling, Mr William C. Eden, Miss Mary Gilliland, Mr Leslie Gunston, Sir Rupert Hart-Davis, Mr Graham Holliday, Mrs Cecil Day Lewis, Dr Kevin McManus, Miss Gillian Nelson, Dr Ellen Sarot, Mr Mark Sinfield, Mr Reresby Sitwell, and Mr George Schlesinger.

I am also much indebted to the John Simon Guggenheim Memorial Foundation for a six months Fellowship, to the staff of the Bodleian Library, the staff of the British Library, Dr Kenneth A. Lohf and the staff of the Columbia University Library, Professor Donald D. Eddy and the staff of the Olin Library at Cornell University, Miss Margaret Weedon and the staff of the English Faculty Library at Oxford, Miss Ellen Dunlap and the staff of the Humanities Research Center of the University of Texas at Austin; to Professor Michael Kammen and Professor Eric Blackall, successive directors of the Society for the Humanities at Cornell, who gave the growing edition a home under their hospitable roof; to Mr Hugo Brunner, Chairman of Chatto & Windus, whose generosity made the book possible; to Mr Ron Costley and Mr Barry Featherstone, who were responsible, respectively, for its design and production; and to its compositors, whose accuracy was a source of admiration, envy, and reproach to a grateful editor.

I must end this as I ended an earlier Foreword, by thanking Mrs Harold

Owen for her continuing encouragement and my wife for accepting the poet as a ghostly addition to the family for so long.

J. H. S.

Cornell University
Ithaca, New York
January 1982

CONTENTS

VOLUME ONE

Biographical Table: Wilfred Owen 1893–1918 xiii
Introduction xxi
List of Abbreviations xxvi

THE POEMS
1 To Poesy 3
2 Written in a Wood, September 1910 7
3 My dearest Colin 8
6 Sonnet/Written at Teignmouth, on a Pilgrimage to Keats's House 10
13 Lines Written on My Nineteenth Birthday 11
14 Supposed Confessions of a Secondrate Sensitive Mind in Dejection 13
18 O believe that God gives you 16
19 Little Claus and Big Claus 17
21 The Rivals 27
22 A Rhymed Epistle to E.L.G. 29
25 The Dread of Falling into Naught 34
26 Science has looked, and sees no life but this 35
31 The Little Mermaid 37
32 The Two Reflections 58
34 Deep under turfy grass and heavy clay 59
35 Unto what pinnacles of desperate heights 60
36 Impromptu/I have none other thought of peace 61
38 Sonnet/Daily I muse on her 63
40 But it is not enough to look upon a rolling main 64
44 Uriconium 65
45 When late I viewed the gardens of rich men 69
53 Long ages past in Egypt thou wert worshipped 70
54 O World of many worlds, O life of lives 71
62 The time was aeon; and the place all earth 73
63 Nocturne 75
64 Impromptu/Now, let me feel 76
65 A Palinode 77
67 It was a navy boy, so prim, so trim 79
68 Whereas most women live this difficult life 81

vii

72 A New Heaven 82
74 Storm 83
75 To the Bitter Sweet-Heart: A Dream 84
78 Roundel/In Shrewsbury Town 85
79 How Do I Love Thee? 86
83 The Fates 87
85 Happiness 88
86 Song of Songs 89
88 Has your soul sipped 90
89 The Swift 92
90 Inspection 95
91 With an Identity Disc 96
94 The Promisers 97
95 Music 98
96 Anthem for Doomed Youth 99
98 Winter Song 101
99 Six O'clock in Princes Street 102
100 The One Remains 103
101 The Sleeping Beauty 104
102 The city lights along the waterside 105
103 Autumnal 106
104 The Unreturning 107
105 Perversity 108
106 Maundy Thursday 109
107 The Peril of Love 110
108 The Poet in Pain 111
109 Whither is passed the softly-vanished day 112
110 On My Songs 113
111 To —— 114
112 To Eros 115
113 1914 116
114 Purple 117
115 On a Dream 118
116 Stunned by their life's explosion into love 119
117 From My Diary, July 1914 120
118 The Ballad of Many Thorns 121
122 I saw his round mouth's crimson deepen as it fell 123
123 Apologia pro Poemate Meo 124
124 Le Christianisme 126
129 Hospital Barge 127

130 Sweet is your antique body, not yet young 129
133 Page Eglantine 130
134 The Rime of the Youthful Mariner 131
135 Who is the god of Canongate 132
136 My Shy Hand 133
137 At a Calvary near the Ancre 134
139 Miners 135
141 The Letter 137
142 Conscious 138
143 Schoolmistress 139
144 Dulce et Decorum Est 140
145 A Tear Song 142
146 The Dead-Beat 144
147 Insensibility 145
148 Strange Meeting 148
149 Sonnet/On Seeing a Piece of Our Heavy Artillery Brought into Action 151
150 Asleep 152
151 Arms and the Boy 154
152 The Show 155
153 Futility 158
154 The End 159
155 S.I.W. 160
157 The Calls 162
158 Training 164
160 The Next War 165
161 Greater Love 166
162 The Last Laugh 168
163 Mental Cases 169
164 The Chances 171
165 The Send-Off 172
166 The Parable of the Old Man and the Young 174
167 Disabled 175
168 A Terre 178
169 The Kind Ghosts 181
170 Soldier's Dream 182
171 I am the ghost of Shadwell Stair 183
173 Elegy in April and September 184
174 Exposure 185
175 The Sentry 188

176 Smile, Smile, Smile 190
177 Spring Offensive 192

VOLUME TWO

THE MANUSCRIPTS OF THE POEMS

THE FRAGMENTS
 4 Before reading a Biography of Keats for the first time 383
 5 Consumption is Consumption 384
 7 Within those days 385
 8 Handling the fairy-strange enchantments 386
 9 Full springs of Thought around me rise 387
10 At Dawn, I love to stray upon the meeting-line 389
11 The West! I dare not pass into the West 390
12 Sonnet/When I perceive, by watching other men's 391
15 Spring not, spring not in my wild eyes, O Tears 393
16 Impressionist 396
17 O, Jesus, now thine own self speaking 397
20 Eve of St. Mark 398
23 Why should the anguish of leaving those we love 399
24 How do the heavens rule my gloomy moods 401
27 Tis but love's shadow—that so haunts my thought 403
28 Hearts and Tarts 407
29 There is a set of men today who deal 409
30 Science Contradicted 410
33 Listen! the multitude is wailing for its sins 412
37 Now, what's your Poet, but a Child of Nine 414
39 Scene: Con Val-Escent Stage of New Monia 417
41 Here all the Summer could I stay 422
42 I Began to Run 423
43 Written On a June Night. (1911) 425
46 All children 428
47 The Imbecile 429
48 Tom Tit 430
49 Completion of "Tonight I have my friar" 431
50 Instead of dew, descended on the moors 433
51 Ballad of the Morose Afternoon 435
52 We two had known each other 437
55 Nights with the Wind. A Rhapsody 439

56 Nous ne nous fions pas à la multitude d'une armée 444
57 A Contemplation 445
58 On seeing a lock of Keat's Hair 446
59 About the winter forest loomed 448
60 The sun, far fallen in the afternoon 449
61 I am to thee a Sunflower to the Sun 451
66 Song/What time I saw her in the budding day 452
69 An Imperial Elegy 453
70 Purgatorial Passions 455
71 It was an evening 457
73 I know that I have paid for every drop of pleasure 458
76 When on the kindling wood the coals are piled 459
77 It was the noiseless hour 460
80 Hide ah! my Flower, hide close 462
81 O piteous mistake: o wrong wrong word 463
82 Perseus 464
84 Ballad of Lady Yolande 472
87 Lines to a Beauty seen in Limehouse 481
92 I know the music 485
93 But I was looking at the permanent stars 487
97 Beauty 489
119 The End 491
120 With those that are become 492
121 Spells & Incantation 494
125 Golden Hair 497
126 The Women & the Slain 500
127 Mourn for the nights not yet begun 510
128 Cramped in that funnelled hole 511
131 Earth's wheels run oiled with blood 514
132 Reunion 518
138 The Wrestlers 520
140 Sunrise 526
156 O true to the old equities and probities 528
159 As bronze maybe much beautified 529
172 The roads also have their wistful rest 531

APPENDIXES

Appendix A Owen's Preface 535
Appendix B Owen's Lists of Contents 537
Appendix C Table of Paper Sizes and Watermarks 541

Index of Titles and First Lines 551

Frontispiece in Volume One
Owen's draft Preface (BL 0.1, reproduced by permission of the British Library). See pp. 535–6 for a transcription
Frontispiece in Volume Two
Fair copy of 'I am the ghost of Shadwell Stair' given to Charles Scott Moncrieff (and reproduced by permission of the Wilfred Owen Collection, Rare Book and Manuscript Library, Columbia University). See p. 360

BIOGRAPHICAL TABLE: Wilfred Owen 1893–1918

Dates of composition and revision will be found under
the texts of individual poems

- 1893 *18 March* Wilfred Edward Salter Owen (WO) born at Plas Wilmot, Oswestry, son of Tom and Susan Owen
- 1895 *30 May* Mary Millard Owen born
- 1897 *16 March* Plas Wilmot sold at Grandfather Shaw's death. Tom Owen appointed to supervisory post at Birkenhead with the Great Western and London and North Eastern Railways
  April Tom Owen applies for transfer; appointed to Shrewsbury
  5 September Harold Owen (HO) born in Canon Street, Shrewsbury
- 1897–8 *Winter* Tom Owen reappointed to Birkenhead. Family moves to 14 Willmer Road, Birkenhead
- 1898 *Spring* Holiday in Ireland
- 1898–9 Move to 7 Elm Grove, Birkenhead, and further move to 51 Milton Street, Birkenhead
- 1900 *11 June* WO starts school (in mid-term) at the Birkenhead Institute
  24 July Colin Shaw Owen (CO) born
- 1902 *Summer* Holiday at Tramore, Ireland
- 1903 or 1904 *Summer* Holiday in Broxton
- 1905 *Summer* Holiday in Scarborough
  August Holiday with the Paton family at Rhewl, Wales
- 1906 *July* Holiday at Torquay and Carbis Bay
  Summer Holiday with the Smallpage family at Waenfawr, Wales
- 1906–7 *Winter* Tom Owen appointed Assistant Superintendent, GW and LNER, Western Region; the family moves to 1 Cleveland Place, Underdale Road, Shrewsbury. WO starts at Shrewsbury Technical School
- 1908 *April* WO stays with the Gunston family in Wimbledon
  June Tom Owen takes WO to Brittany
- 1909 *July* WO goes again to Brittany with his father, then to Torquay

1910 *January* The family moves to Mahim, Monkmoor Road, Shrewsbury
August WO and HO on holiday in Torquay. WO calls on Miss Christabel Coleridge, granddaughter of the poet
1911 *April* WO again on holiday in Torquay; reads Sidney Colvin's *Keats* and visits Teignmouth
Summer Works as a pupil-teacher at the Wyle Cop School, Shrewsbury, while preparing for matriculation exam
9 September Takes University of London matriculation exam. Visits British Museum to see Keats manuscripts
28 September Interview with the Revd Herbert Wigan, vicar of Dunsden, near Reading. Is offered an unpaid post as lay assistant and pupil in this Evangelical parish
Early October Hears he has matriculated, but not with honours
20 October Arrives at Dunsden
1912 *16 April* Arranges to take botany classes at University College, Reading, for six hours a week
June Meets Miss Edith Morley, head of the English Department, University College
8 July Joins family at Pringle Bank, Kelso, for holiday with the Bulman family
20–25 July Attends Keswick Convention
December Miss Morley urges him to sit for a scholarship to University College, Reading, and invites him to attend her remaining classes in Old English free of charge
Christmas At Shrewsbury
28 December Visits Mr Morgan, a clergyman at Bordesley, Birmingham, and is offered another post as lay assistant, which he does not accept. Returns to Dunsden
1913 *Early January* Determines to leave Dunsden and to break with Evangelical religion
7 February Returns to Shrewsbury
February–March Ill with congestion of the lungs
13 March HO joins the Merchant Service and sails for the Mediterranean and India
18 April–3 May Convalescent holiday in Torquay. Starts to look for teaching post
16–19 May Takes the Reading University scholarship
July HO returns to England
c. 6 July Hears he has failed to win the Reading scholarship

August Holiday with Uncle Edward Quayle's family at Dorfold, Great Meols, Cheshire

c. 15 September To Bordeaux, to teach English at the Berlitz School of Languages. Lodges in rue Castelmoron

28 September Moves into room at 95 rue Porte Dijeaux

Mid-October Visited in Bordeaux by Tom Owen

November Ill with gastro-enteritis

1913–14 *Winter* HO again at sea in the South Atlantic, remaining at sea, with occasional short leaves, until autumn 1916

1914 *18 March* Twenty-first birthday

25 July Gives up job at the Berlitz School

31 July To Castel Lorenzo, Bagnères-de-Bigorre, High Pyrenees, as tutor to Mme Léger, a Berlitz pupil

4 August War declared. French government moves to Bordeaux

c. 21 August Meets the poet Laurent Tailhade

24 August Invited by Mme Léger to go with her to Canada in March 1915

17 September Returns to Bordeaux with the Légers, and stays with them at 12 rue Blanc-Dutrouilh. Starts to look for pupils as a free-lance teacher of English

7 October Moves to temporary lodgings with the family of a pupil, Raoul Lem, at 12 rue St. Louis, Bordeaux

12 October Mme Léger leaves for Canada

19 October Moves to new lodgings at 31 rue Desfourniels

4 December Offered post as tutor to the two elder de la Touche boys at the Châlet, Mérignac, near Bordeaux

8 December Accepts post for a month, retaining his private pupils and going to Mérignac in the afternoons

19 December Moves to Mérignac to live at the Châlet

1915 *Early January* Channel considered unsafe. Invited to stay at Mérignac until the spring

10 April Miss de la Touche, the boys' aunt, decides to keep them in France and urges WO to stay

18 May To Imperial Hotel, Russell Square, London, while carrying out a commission at the British Industries Fair for a Bordeaux scent manufacturer, then to Shrewsbury for a short visit

13 June Returns to Bordeaux via Le Havre and Paris. Into new lodgings at 18 rue Beaubadat, continuing to teach the de

la Touche boys as well as his Bordeaux pupils
20 June Considers joining the Artists' Rifles in the autumn, after returning the boys to Downside School
10 July Considers joining the Italian Cavalry if he is unable to join the Artists' Rifles
31 August Gives up lodgings to return to England; persuaded to stay on three more weeks, and finds new lodgings at 1 Place St. Christoly, Bordeaux
14 September To London with Johnny and Bobbie de la Touche
15 September Sees the boys off to Downside from Paddington and goes home to Shrewsbury
21 October Joins up in the Artists' Rifles. Into lodgings at Les Lilas, 54 Tavistock Square, W.C.
27 October Meets Harold Monro at the Poetry Bookshop, 35 Devonshire Street, W.1
15 November To Hare Hall Camp, Gidea Park, Essex, as Cadet Owen, Artists' Rifles

1916 *c. 1 January* Home on a week's leave
27 February–5 March Ten days' course in London; lodgings over the Poetry Bookshop
4 March Shows poems to Monro
5 March To Officers' School, Balgores House, Gidea Park
19 May On leave, first in London and then in Shrewsbury, pending gazette
4 June Commissioned into the Manchester Regiment
18 June Reports to 5th (Reserve) Battalion, Manchester Regiment, at Milford Camp, near Witley, Surrey
7 July Attached for a musketry course to 25th Battalion, Middlesex Regiment, Talavera Barracks, Aldershot
Mid-July Weekend leave at Kidmore End, near Reading, home of cousin Leslie Gunston (ELG). To church at Dunsden and sees Revd Wigan
Early August To Mytchett Musketry Camp, Farnborough, in command of the 5th Manchesters contingent
Early September Applies for transfer to Royal Flying Corps; interviewed in London, but is not transferred
14 September Visit from HO
24 September 5th Manchesters move to Oswestry, under canvas

19–20 October 5th Manchesters to Southport, Lancashire, the officers in Queen's Hotel. WO has lodgings for a few days at 168a Lord Street
c. 5 November To the firing ranges at Fleetwood in command of the battalion and brigade firing parties. Lodgings at 111 Bold Street, Fleetwood
8 December Back to Southport
Christmas Embarkation leave
29 December To France and Base Camp, Étaples

1917 *1–2 January* Joins 2nd Manchesters on the Somme near Beaumont Hamel, in a rest area. Assumes command of 3 Platoon, A Coy.
6 January 2nd Manchesters on the move towards front
9–16 January Holds dug-out in no man's land; sentry blinded
20 January Into line again; platoon exposed in severe frost
4 February Arrives at Abbeville for a course on transport duties.
25 February Leaves Abbeville
1 March Rejoins battalion near Fresnoy; posted to B Coy.
14/15 March Concussion following fall at Le Quesnoy-en-Santerre
15 March Evacuated to Military Hospital at Nesle
17 March Moved to 13th Casualty Clearing Station at Gailly
4 April Rejoins battalion at Selency.
8 April Battalion is relieved, and pulls back to Beauvois
12 April Into the line again at Savy Wood for 12 days
21 April 14th Brigade relieved; into cellar quarters at Quivières
2 May Evacuated to 13th CCS with shell-shock
11 June To No. 1 General Hospital, Etretat
16 June To Welsh Hospital, Netley, Hampshire
26 June Arrives at Craiglockhart War Hospital, Slateford, near Edinburgh
Early July Visited by Susan Owen
17 July Writes first contribution to *The Hydra*; becomes editor
Late July Siegfried Sassoon (SS) arrives at Craiglockhart
30 July Talks to 'Field Club' on 'Do Plants Think?'
c. 17 August Introduces himself to SS
1 September 'Song of Songs' published in *The Hydra*
25 September Gives first of several lessons in English literature

at Tynecastle School, Edinburgh; appears before Medical Board

13 October Introduced by SS to Robert Graves, who is shown draft of 'Disabled'

28 October Appears before Medical Board; three weeks' leave pending return to unit

3 November To London

4 November To Shrewsbury

9 November Lunches and dines with Robert Ross at the Reform Club and meets Arnold Bennett and H. G. Wells

10 November Dines again with Ross, Wells, and Bennett and meets A. G. Gardiner, editor of the *Daily News*

11 November Visits ELG near Winchester

14 November Sees Monro at the Poetry Bookshop

24 November Joins 5th Manchesters at Scarborough for light duties; appointed 'major-domo' of the Officers' Mess, Clarence Gardens Hotel

4 December Promoted Lieutenant

19–23 December Short leave; to Edinburgh, revisiting Craiglockhart and Tynecastle School

Christmas SS posted back to France

1918 *23 January* Attends Graves's marriage to Nancy Nicholson at St James's Piccadilly. Meets Charles Scott Moncrieff

26 January 'Miners' published in *The Nation*

12 March To Northern Command Depot, Ripon

c. 23 March Into lodgings at 7 Borrage Lane, Ripon

9–11 April Weekend leave in Shrewsbury and last meeting with HO

22 April Upgraded to Division 4

10 May Upgraded to Division 3

Mid-May 'Song of Songs' published in *The Bookman*

16–19 May In London, staying in flat over Ross's in Half Moon Street. Visits War Office; meets Osbert Sitwell at Ross's flat

21 May Upgraded to Division 2

4 June Graded fit for general service

5 June Rejoins 5th Manchesters at Scarborough

11 June Request from Edith and Osbert Sitwell for poems to include in *Wheels 1918*

15 June 'Hospital Barge' and 'Futility' published in *The Nation*

Mid-June CO joins the R.A.F.
13 July SS wounded and invalided home
Mid-July HO sails to join the light cruiser *Astraea* at Simonstown
12–18 August Embarkation leave; sees SS in hospital in London; spends evening with SS and Osbert Sitwell
31 August Reports again to Base Camp, Étaples
9 September To Reception Depot, Amiens, to await arrival of 2nd Manchesters
15 September 2nd Manchesters arrive at Amiens
29 September–3 October Successful assault on Beaurevoir-Fonsomme line. Awarded M.C.
5 October Battalion back to rest area at Hancourt. Robert Ross dies in London
29 October At St. Souplet, into line for the last time
30–31 October Battalion takes over the line west of the Oise-Sambre Canal, near Ors, in preparation for an attack across the canal at dawn on 4 November
4 November Killed in early morning on the canal bank
11 November News of WO's death reaches Shrewsbury. Armistice signed

INTRODUCTION

The poems of Wilfred Owen present an editor with uncommon problems that call for uncommon solutions. He lived to see only four in print: 'Song of Songs' in *The Hydra* and *The Bookman*; 'Miners', 'Futility', and 'Hospital Barge' in *The Nation*. Six months before his death, he told his mother: 'I am to have my work typed at once, and send it to Heinemann, who is certain to send it to [Robert] Ross to read for him!!'[1] No such typescript has ever come to light, but it is hard to believe that any poet capable of writing 'Exposure', 'Strange Meeting', or 'Spring Offensive' would be content to leave such poems in the form in which they have passed to posterity – manuscripts much corrected and, in many cases, clearly unfinished. In the absence of a final typescript, however, an editor must do what he can with what he has.

Siegfried Sassoon and Edith Sitwell were the first to thread their way through the maze of manuscripts. Sassoon's 1920 edition of Owen's *Poems* contained 23 poems and fragments, and a 24th was added for the 1921 reissue. Edmund Blunden's 1931 edition added 35 more, though 2 were halves of the same poem, and his notes quoted another 2 in full. In 1963, C. Day Lewis penetrated deeper into the maze for his edition of *The Collected Poems*, and published a further 19 for the first time. In his Introduction he wrote: 'In general, my text will not often be found to differ greatly from Blunden's.' But over the years the need for a radical review of the text became increasingly clear to scholars and critics, among them Dr Dominic Hibberd, whose 1973 selection, *Wilfred Owen / War Poems and Others*, departed from Day Lewis's text (of the 55 poems the two had in common) at more than 60 points. Hibberd wished to depart more radically still, but was discouraged by the copyright holders and publishers, on the grounds that the present edition was already in preparation.

The major problem confronting Owen's editors has not been the legibility of his manuscripts – though some are difficult, some impossible to read – but their chronology. In deciding the sequence of drafts and choosing those that show the poet's latest revisions, my distinguished predecessors had to rely almost exclusively on internal evidence. I have been more fortunate, first, in having the benefit of their skilled reading of such evidence; secondly, in having access not only to all the verse manuscripts, which are mainly undated, but to all of Owen's letters, which are mainly dated.[2] This has made possible an analysis of their paper, which

1 *Wilfred Owen/Collected Letters*, edited by Harold Owen and John Bell (1967), 552.
2 There are major collections of the verse manuscripts in the Manuscript Students' Room of

has shed light on many of the darker places of the maze. Scrutiny of the verse manuscripts revealed 22 different watermarks (2 of them in paper with both a larger and a smaller size), 16 of which are to be found in dated letters. The manuscripts and letters also have in common several varieties of paper lacking a watermark, but distinct in size, colour, and texture; though there are occasional variations in size between sheets from the same 'batch' of paper, either because the manufacturer did not precisely align the sheets before guillotining (some are not cut square), or because the poet halved or otherwise cropped his page. Appendix C, on pp. 541–50, sets out in its table of paper sizes and watermarks much, but by no means all, of the evidence for dating the manuscripts. Other clues are to be found in letters, and in the matching of ink, pencil, and handwriting. There is, for example, the case of Owen's capital I's. These tend to be curved like a closing bracket $)$ until, in August 1914, he switches to J, which he employs until May 1915 when he changes to the simpler $|$. All such evidence must, of course, be used with caution. There is a great deal of it, however, and most of it is both mutually supportive and supported by – or not at variance with – internal evidence yielded by the text.

The result of all this is a much more complicated chronology. Where editors and critics have tended to speak of individual poems as 'early' or 'late', many can now be seen to have been written over a considerable period; like 'Exposure' (No. 174), begun in December 1917, revised in early 1918, and further revised that September. The case of 'Exposure' is the more cautionary in that one of its manuscripts appears to be dated 'Feb. 1916'. Other of Owen's own dates on his manuscripts turn out to be misleading, particularly dates in titles such as 'Written on a June Night (1911)' (No. 43) or 'From My Diary, 1914' (No. 117). The discovery – on unarguable watermark evidence – that the latter poem was written in 1917/18, rather than 1914, radically alters the received view of Owen's development of parahyme.[3]

With the dating of individual manuscripts, there became apparent the need not only for a thorough overhaul of the texts of poems previously published, but for further exploration and exposition of the intricate 'root

---

the British Library in London and the English Faculty Library at Oxford. A few other manuscripts, detailed in the text, are in private hands. Most of the letters are held in the Humanities Research Center of the University of Texas. Those to Leslie Gunston were presented by him to the English Faculty Library at Oxford; seven to Siegfried Sassoon are in the Columbia University Library; and a few to the other recipients are in private hands.

3 See, for example, Dennis Welland, *Wilfred Owen / A Critical Study* (1960; revised and enlarged, 1978), 112–13.

system' underlying the published and the unpublished. Critics have noted the connections between the fragments, 'All Sounds have been as Music' and 'Bugles Sang',[4] and 'Anthem for Doomed Youth' (No. 96), and a number of similar connections appear in the following pages. Many fragments, of course, have no such connections – or none that I have detected – and some have little or no literary merit. Why then was it decided to print them? To present for the first time a map of Owen's poetic development, this edition offers in one chronological sequence the latest text of every poem and fragment. The poems appear first; an account of their manuscripts, second; and the fragments third. To those readers who ask whether Owen would have wanted it this way, one can only reply that it is hard to imagine the poet who would discourage a serious interest in his poems; or who would think it logical to print all his letters and fragments of letters but not all his poems and fragments of poems.

The edition, which has been divided into two volumes to enable readers to have text, notes, and manuscript material before them at the same time, is organized as follows:

THE POEMS (pp. 1–194)

Poems and fragments alike are numbered and ordered by date of final revision rather than first composition. Since the text in each case reflects the poet's latest intentions, it would have been misleading to place the poems and fragments in a chronology determined by his earliest intentions. The successive stages of composition are detailed and dated in the notes following each poem. Problems remain, of course, such as the dates of composition of the sonnets (Nos. 100–16) revised and fair-copied, probably for Sassoon at Craiglockhart in October–November 1917, or conceivably at Scarborough between November 1917 and January 1918. 'The Unreturning' is known to have been begun in 1912/13, 'The Sleeping Beauty' in 1914, and others may be as early or earlier. Following an account of the date, place, and circumstances of composition, the notes on each poem offer any information relevant to its biographical, historical, and literary context.

To avoid excessive repetition of material, I give frequent page references to my biography, *Wilfred Owen* (1974), in the notes. Those references printed in bold face are to photo-facsimiles of manuscripts reproduced in the biography. Some dates assigned to poems and fragments in this edition

---

[4] In this edition, where untitled fragments are titled by their first line, these appear respectively as 'I know the music' (No. 92) and 'But I was looking at the permanent stars' (No. 93).

differ from those given in the biography, and should be understood to supersede them.

By the standard that defines an unfinished poem as a fragment, many of Owen's would be classed as fragmentary. If some of the decisions I have made in this respect appear arbitrary, supporting facts will be found in or accompanying the transcripts of the manuscripts.

THE MANUSCRIPTS OF THE POEMS (pp. 195–379)

The notes to each poem make reference to a later page, in volume II, at which the manuscript or manuscripts are described and in some cases transcribed. There, in a headnote, will be found, first, a reference to the poem's appearance in a magazine, in those few cases where the text there printed *has the poet's authority*, and then in the editions of Sassoon, Blunden, Day Lewis, and Hibberd. As these latter have no such authority, no textual collation is offered, although the more important departures from Day Lewis's text are recorded in the notes. The sequence of manuscripts (and, on occasion, typescripts) is then set out chronologically; the last listed being the copy-text unless stated to the contrary. A manuscript folio is to be regarded as a recto unless described as 'v' (verso).

In the case of pre-1914 poems (Nos. 1–45), an apparatus criticus lists any significant substantive variants from the copy-text. Spelling and punctuation have been silently emended. To have supplied these early poems with the complete apparatus necessary for the later poems would have doubled the cost, but not the value, of an already expensive book.

In the case of 1914–18 poems (Nos. 53–177), all variants from the copy-text are recorded except when a full transcript of the manuscript is given. Where manuscripts other than copy-text – of poems either early or late – shed light on the genesis of the work, transcripts of these in chronological sequence (earliest first) follow a line of five spaced dots dividing such subsidiary material from the treatment of the copy-text.

All transcripts distinguish between ink (printed in light face type) and pencil or crayon (printed in semi-bold). Where, for example, the word 'That' in ink has been changed in pencil to 'The', the emendation will appear as Th$^{e}_{at}$. An illegible word in ink will be rendered as [?]; an illegible word in ink cancelled in pencil as **{?}**; an illegible word in pencil cancelled in ink as {?}. Special solutions to special problems – such as interlinear emendations by Sassoon to poems Nos. 96 and 139 – are detailed as they occur.

THE FRAGMENTS (pp. 381–532)
The latest version of each fragmentary poem is presented in a transcript conforming to the conventions outlined above, and with notes comparable to those on the completed poems. Where an earlier version or versions illuminate/s this or another poem/fragment, it or they follow a line of five spaced dots.

While it is unlikely that any more poems by Wilfred Owen will come to light, some fragments may. The whereabouts of certain manuscripts cited in this edition are unknown. The poet's mother and his brother Harold each, on occasion, gave manuscripts to friends.[5]

On New Year's Eve 1917, Owen wrote: 'I go out of this year a Poet, my dear Mother, as which I did not enter it. I am held peer by the Georgians; I am a poet's poet.'[6] Subsequent years have proved him right. After the recognition of his contemporaries, Graves, Sassoon, the Sitwells, came the recognition of the poets of the Thirties, Auden, Day Lewis, and Spender. The major editions of Owen's poems have all been undertaken by poets. Whether this has been to their advantage it is not for me to say, but I like to think the young man proud to be 'a poet's poet' would have approved, and would perhaps have been tolerant of the errors inevitable in the fulfilment of a task involving many thousands of decisions.

Owen was fascinated by Keats's manuscripts. Other more recent poets have studied with profit to their poems the posthumously published manuscripts of Eliot and Yeats, and it is to the poets of tomorrow that I dedicate this happy labour of ten years.

[5] See, for example, the transcripts (made from photocopies), on pp. 319 and 343–4 of MSS given to the late Vera Howland. The following fragments, quoted by Mr Patric Dickinson in an unpublished radio script, 'Wilfred Owen' (transmitted 17 August 1953), were not to be found in the Owen family archive twenty years later:

Fresh was the moon
Shining through the shievéd corn
Autumn that moment born

The dew was like a silver net
Over the lawns and level wet. . . .

The sky-scouring wings of the south—
    summoned wind in wintertide. . . .

[6] *Collected Letters*, 521.

LIST OF ABBREVIATIONS

WO	Wilfred Owen	HO	Harold Owen (brother)
CDL	C. Day Lewis	MO	Mary Owen (sister)
CO	Colin Owen (brother)	OS	Osbert Sitwell
DH	Dominic Hibberd	SO	Susan Owen (mother)
EB	Edmund Blunden	SS	Siegfried Sassoon
ELG	Leslie Gunston		

PRINCIPAL MANUSCRIPT LOCATIONS

BL 0   British Library Additional MS 43720
BL 1   British Library Additional MS 43721
Bod   Bodleian Library, Oxford
CU   Columbia University Library, MS collection
OEF   English Faculty Library, Oxford
OEF/ELG   MS presented by Leslie Gunston to the English Faculty Library, Oxford
OEF/HO   MS or book presented by Mrs Harold Owen to the English Faculty Library, Oxford
OEF/VH   MS presented to the late Miss Vera Howland and since presumed lost; photographic print held in the English Faculty Library, Oxford
Ren   MS presented to Osbert Sitwell; now in the possession of Mr Reresby Sitwell at Renishaw
Tex   Humanities Research Center, University of Texas at Austin. (Numbers following 'Tex' correspond to letter numbers in CL.)

PRINCIPAL PUBLISHED SOURCES

By Wilfred Owen:

CDL   *The Collected Poems of Wilfred Owen*, edited with an Introduction and Notes by C. Day Lewis (London, 1963)
CL   *Wilfred Owen / Collected Letters*, edited by Harold Owen and John Bell (London, 1967)
DH   *Wilfred Owen / War Poems and Others*, edited with an Introduction and Notes by Dominic Hibberd (London, 1973)
EB   *The Poems of Wilfred Owen*, edited with a Memoir by Edmund Blunden (London, 1931)
SS   Wilfred Owen, *Poems*, with an Introduction by Siegfried Sassoon (London, 1920)

Other sources:

Bäckman   Sven Bäckman, *Tradition Transformed / Studies in the Poetry of Wilfred Owen* (Lund, Sweden, 1979)
JFO   Harold Owen, *Journey from Obscurity*, 3 vols. (London, 1963–5)
N&Q   *Notes and Queries*
RES   *Review of English Studies*
Welland   Dennis Welland, *Wilfred Owen / A Critical Study*, revised and enlarged edition (London, 1978)
WO   Jon Stallworthy, *Wilfred Owen* (London, 1974)

All other locations and sources are given in full in the text.

THE POEMS

TO POESY

A thousand suppliants stand around thy throne,
Stricken with love for thee, O Poesy.
I stand among them, and with them I groan,
And stretch my arms for help. Oh, pity me!
No man (save them thou gav'st the right to ascend
And sit with thee, 'nointing with unction fine,
Calling thyself their servant and their friend)
Has loved thee with a purer love than mine.
For, as thou yieldest thy fair self so free
To Masters not a few, so wayward men
Give half their adoration up to thee,
Beseech another goddess guide their pen,
And with another muse their pleasure take.
Not so with me! I neither cease to love,
Nor am content to love but for the sake
Of passing pleasures caught from thee above.
For some will listen to thy trembling voice
Since in its mournful music warbling low,
Or in its measured chants, or bubbling joys
They hear belovèd tunes of long ago.
And some are but enamoured of thy grace
And find it well to kneel to thee, and pray,
Because there oft-times play upon thy face
Smiles of an earthly maiden far away.

Before the eyes of all thou hast the power
To spread Elysium. Gorgeous memories
Of days far distant in the past can flower
Afresh beneath thy touch; yet not for these
Thy mighty spells I love and hymn thy name;
Nor yet because thou know'st the unseen road
Which leads unto the awful halls of Fame,
Where, midst the heapèd honours, thine the load
Most richly prized, of all the crowns the best!
No! not for these I long to win thee, Sweet!
No more is this my fervent, hopeless quest –
To stand among the great ones there, to meet
The bards of old and greet them as my peers.

O impious thought! O I am mad to ask
E'en that their voice may ever reach my ears.

40   Yet show thou me the task,
That shall, as years advance, give power and skill,
Firm hands; an eye which takes all beauty in,
That I may woo thee thus, if thus thy will.
Ah, gladly would I on such task begin
45 But that I know this learning must be bought
With gold as well as toil, and gold I lack.
What then? Dost bid me first seek out the Court
Where this world's wretched god, the money-sack,
Doles out his favours to the cringing herd,
50 There slave for him awhile to earn his pelf?

E'en should I leave him soon, my heart is stirred
With glorious fear and trembles in itself,
When I look forth upon the vasty seas
Of learning to be travelled o'er.
                                I fain
55 Would know the hills, the founts, the very trees,
Where sang the Greeks of old. I would have plain
Before my vision, heroes, poets, kings,
Hear their clear accents; then observe where trod
E'en mythic men; yea, next on Hermes' wings
60 Would mount Olympus and discern each god.

All this to speed my suit with Poesy
Meseems must do; and far, far more than this;
In divers tongues my thoughts must flow out free;
And, in my own tongue, with no word amiss,
65 For all its writers must be known to me.
My hand must wield the critic's weapons, too,
To save myself, or strike an enemy.
Oh grant that this long training ne'er undo
My simple, ardent love! Throw early dews
70 Of inspiration oft-times on my brow.
Let them fall suddenly and darkly as thou choose,
Uncertain, fitful as the thunder-drops
Which sprinkle us then cease, to splash once more

  Rapidly round, still pausing for long stops,
75 Not knowing if to vent their heavy store
  Upon the parching ground, or wait awhile
  Till hasty travelling winds bring increased worth.
  But as at last the concentrated pile
  Of seething vapours flings its might to earth
80 In spurts of fire and rain, and to the ground
  Flashes its energy, yields up its very soul,
  So, midst long triumph-roars of awful sound,
  Flash thou thy soul to me at last, and roll
  Torrential streams of thought upon my brain,
85 So give, yea give Thyself to me
  At last.
  We shall be happy, thou and I. In me
  Thou'lt find a jealous guardian of thy charms,
  A doting master, leaving all to be
90 Ever with thee, ever in thine arms.
  Forget my youth, forget my ignorance,
  Spurn not my lowliness, and lack of friends
  Who might help on my progress and perchance
  Present me fearless at the throne where bends
95 Full timidly my lonely being now.
  Friends' service would be naught if thine own hand
  Uplifted me; do not thine eyes endow
  Far brighter wealth than books, and far more grand?
  Then come! Come with a rushing impulse swift,
100 Or draw near slowly, gently, so it be
  Never to part.
      Round us the world may drift,
  Some with scoffs and frowns, with laughter some:
  Their hateful mockery I shall not heed.
  How could I feel ashamed to stand with one
105 Who deigns to stoop and be my life's high meed?
  Yet if I would not for its jeering shun
  The world, no more would I parade its courts
  To change those jeers to applause by showing men
  Thy power. Publicity but poorly sorts
110 My sacred joy, if thou should'st guide my pen.

Loath would I be to show my exceeding bliss

      Even to closest friends. But all unseen,
      And far from men's gaze would I feel thy kiss;
      No witness save the speechless star-lamps keen
115 When thou stoop'st over me. No eye
      But Cynthia's look on us, when through the night
      We sit alone, our faces pressing nigh,
      Quietly shining in her quiet light.

Written probably in 1909–10, this supplication to the muse owes much to Keats's 'The Fall of Hyperion' (wo, 53–4).

TITLE Cp. Tennyson, 'To Poesy'.
    52 glorious fear: Cp. No. 54, 'O World of many worlds, O life of lives' (p. 71), l. 33: 'O glorious fear!'
116–18 Cp. Coleridge, 'Frost at Midnight', l. 74: 'Quietly shining to the quiet Moon'.

MS, p. 197

WRITTEN IN A WOOD, SEPTEMBER 1910

Full ninety autumns hath this ancient beech
Helped with its myriad leafy tongues to swell
The dirges of the deep-toned western gale,
And ninety times hath all its power of speech
5   Been stricken dumb, at sound of winter's yell,
Since Adonais, no more strong and hale,
Might have rejoiced to linger here and teach
His thoughts in sonnets to the listening dell;
Or glide in fancy through those leafy grots
10 And bird-pavilions hung with arras green,
To hear the sonnets of its minstrel choir.
Ah, ninety times again, when autumn rots
Shall birds and leaves be mute and all unseen,
Yet shall I see fair Keats, and hear his lyre.

Written – as indicated by its title – in September 1910, this sonnet testifies to WO's early admiration for the poems of Keats and Shelley (wo, 53).

    1 Full ninety autumns: Keats died in Rome on 21 February 1821.
    6 Adonais: Shelley's name for Keats in his pastoral elegy with that title.
    9 those leafy grots: Cp. Keats, *Endymion*, ii. 921: 'the lofty grot'.

MS, p. 197

3   My dearest Colin,
       How glad I was to have your little letter,
       To know your throat is really, truly better.
       (My words, you see, are falling into verse-gear,
5   I hope it will not make you any worse, dear!)

       About your new Bird's Egg Book worth six shillings
       What *can* I say until myself I see it?
       But now it's bought so dearly, so dearly
                        so dearly
10   O carefully use it!
       Oh brown-paper-bind it!
       Or you'll certainly lose it,
       Yes, and *I*'ll find it!
                        (Oh really!
15   Oh really!)
       Then you'll see it never more
       So don't you leave it on the floor!
                        (D'you hear me,
                        D'you hear me?)
20   Now let me tell you something of my doings –
       We all went out to tea last night to Painter's
       And played a game I know you'd like to play at:
       We shot an air-gun at a target on their door
       And even Vera did her level best to score.
25   Hence excepting Auntie (for such sports too aged)
       We might have been all *Bis(i)ley* engaged.
       That afternoon we also saw the 'Pictures'.
       The French boys always charm me, but the mixtures
       Of Blood and Thunder Stories sometimes shock me.
30   How does Mary like her Book of Botany?
       I wish I could find some Pheasant's Eggs or Partridges
       To bring you; but I got you lots of empty cartridges.

P.S.		
35	'There was a boy so wondrous wise	⎫
	He tried to see his nose	⎬
	And turning inwards both his eyes	⎪
	He now in glasses goes: – '	⎭
	must now be *changed to*	
	'There is a boy of Shrewsbury	⎫
40	On whom all doctors dote,	⎬
	He lets them take hot iodine	⎪
	And burn out half his throat.'	⎭

Written at Alpenrose, the Oxfordshire home of WO's uncle, Jack Gunston, on 1 January 1911 to CO.

    21 Painter's: On 29 December 1910, WO had written to SO: 'Tomorrow we are all going to the Painters' to tea. This Mr. Painter was formerly a school-master and is now in a G.W.R. office.' (CL, 66)

    24 Vera: WO's cousin, Vera Gunston.

    26 *Bis(i)ley*: The National Rifle Association held its Imperial Meeting each July at Bisley Camp in Surrey.

    36 glasses: CO had new spectacles.

    40–1 CO had tonsillitis.

MS, p. 198

6 SONNET
Written at Teignmouth, on a Pilgrimage to Keats's House

Three colours have I known the Deep to wear;
'Tis well today that Purple grandeurs gloom,
Veiling the Emerald sheen and Sky-blue glare.
Well, too, that lowly-brooding clouds now loom
5 In sable majesty around, fringed fair
With ermine-white of surf: to me they bear
Watery memorials of His mystic doom
Whose Name was writ in Water (saith his tomb).

Eternally may sad waves wail his death,
10 Choke in their grief 'mongst rocks where he has lain,
Or heave in silence, yearning with hushed breath,
While mournfully trail the slow-moved mists and rain,
And softly the small drops slide from weeping trees,
Quivering in anguish to the sobbing breeze.

Begun on 21 April 1911 at Teignmouth – where Keats had lived from March to May 1818 at 20 Northumberland Place (formerly 20 the Strand) – this sonnet was finished at Shrewsbury shortly afterwards (WO, 57–**8**).

> 8 On Keats's instructions, his tombstone in Rome bears the words: 'Here lies one whose name was writ in water.'

MSS, p. 198

LINES WRITTEN ON MY NINETEENTH BIRTHDAY
March 18, 1912

Two Spirits woke me from my sleep this morn;
Both most unwelcome were; for they have torn
Away from me the shady screens of ease
And unreflecting, unself-scanning Peace
Wherein I used to hide me from annoy
In years which found and left me still a Boy.
The First rose solemn, with a Voice of stern
Monition; and it said: 'Look back! and learn
To number life by moments, not by years;
Know that thy youth to its completion nears.
This night the final minute hath been laid
Upon thy nineteen Springs. Aye, be dismayed
To see the Fourth Part of thy utmost Span
Now spent! What then? Affrighted dost thou plan
To crowd the Rest with Action, every whit?
Ev'n so essay; but know thou canst not knit
Thy web of hours so close as to regain
E'en one lost stitch! For ever gaps remain!'
Hereat it ceased; for now a second Shade
Caught all my senses to't; no sound it made;
No form it had; but quietly it drew
Its tightening hand of Pain through every thew
Of my frail body. . . . Pain? – Why Pain today?
Sure, not a taste of what this tingling clay
Shall suffer through the year? And yet, if so,
'Twill be but my most rightful share, I trow,
Scarce worse than the keen hunger-pinch that racks
Numberless wretches all their life. Pain slacks
Its hold on one, only to grasp another;
And why should I be spared, and not my brother?

So thinking, quickly I pass the day. And lo!
What kindnesses the Friends around me show!
How many eyes in warm solicitude
Have smiled upon me! Tongues that have been rude
Are gentle now. . . . Yet still, how do I miss
Thine eyes, *thy* voice, my Mother! Oft I kiss

Thy portrait, and I clutch thy letter dear
As if it were thy hand.
                    At this, fresh cheer
Comes over me; and now upon my couch
40 Of ruby velvet, o'er the fire I crouch
In full content. I only pause from reading
To scribble these few lines; or, scarcely heeding
The dismal damp abroad, to mock the rain
Shooting its sleety balls at me in vain.
45 – Ho, thus, methinks, hereafter, when the weak
Creations of a Mental Mist shall seek
To quench my soul, I'll thwart them by the shield
Of crystal Hope!
                    For there have been revealed
Heart-secrets since the coming of this day,
50 Making me thankful for its thorn-paved way.
Among them this: 'No joy is comparable
Unto the *Melting* – soft and gradual –
Of Torture's needles in the flesh. To sail
Smoothly from out the abysmal anguish-jail
55 And tread the placid plains of *normal ease*
Is sweeter far, I deem, than all the glees
Which we may catch by mounting higher still
Into the dangerous air where actual Bliss doth thrill.'

Written at Dunsden on 18 March 1912 (WO, 71), these lines accompanied WO's letter of 19 March to SO: 'But on my birthday morning I was awakened by the unrelenting gnawings [of indigestion] within, and took a bit of toast for breakfast. The couch from the passage was then brought down for me, and thereon I lay all day; finding relief however very soon after breakfast-time. To ease me, I employed my time upon the "lines", which you have, with the ink, as it were, still wet upon them. . . . Don't be content with a first reading but if you fail to see any point at all, 'tis no fault of yours. Consider how quickly I wrote!' (CL, 125)

    36–7 Cp. Cowper, 'On the Receipt of my Mother's Picture out of Norfolk', ll. 1–4:
>Oh that those lips had language! Life has pass'd
>With me but roughly since I heard thee last.
>Those lips are thine – thy own sweet smiles I see,
>The same that oft in childhood solaced me . . .

MSS, p. 199

SUPPOSED CONFESSIONS
OF A SECONDRATE SENSITIVE MIND
IN DEJECTION

Time was when I have loved the bards whose strains
Saddened the heart, and wrought a heavy mood;
Aye, and my spirit felt a joy to brood
O'er melodies which told of ancient pains.
5   Lovely the tones when poet's lips have moved
For very mournfulness. . . . O fair the sight
(As now we see it) of a Spirit bright
Bowed on a southern strand; his work approved
Of none; his name despised or else unknown.
10 O then, how firm and close was his embrace
Unto Despondency! – Her shadowed face,
Methought, how fair! What music in her moan!
Ye, too, have sometimes wished her near;
Loved a chill dampness round thy path, and known
15 Her voice, which like a weary wind and lone,
Fled through the woods with lamentation drear.
But think not, if your life-blood still is warm,
That ye have looked upon Despondency.
Ye have but seen her in another's eye,
20 As Perseus fearfully beheld the form
Of Gorgon, mirrored in the stilly well.
There may ye guess the beauty of that Head,
The pallor and the mystery – but the Dread
Ye feel not, nor the horror, nor the spell.

25 But, face to face, she fixed on me her stare:
Woe, woe, my blood has never moved since then;
Down-dragged like corpse in sucking, slimy fen,
I sank to feel the breath of that Despair.

With Autumn mists, and hand in hand with Night,
30 She came to me. But at the break of day,
Went not again, but stayed, and yet doth stay.
' – O Horror, doth not Pain take note of light
And darkness, – doth he not hold off betimes,
And yield his victim for an hour to Sleep?

35   Then why dost thou, O Curst, the long night steep
     In bloodiness and stains of shadowy crimes?'
     She hears my cry, and mutters yet,
     'No rest, no rest for thee, O Slave of mine';
     Till I do hate myself and would resign
40   My life to pay a murderer's awful debt.

     Out, out to moorlands, from such thoughts I flee
     And seek the balm that fair fresh woods distil.
     There find I all things in a hushèd thrill
     For dread of that grey fiend that walks with me.

45   She leads me forth, and poisons autumn eves
     With hellish scenes; shows me an aged tree
     Bending and groaning in its agony
     Before a wind tormenting it for leaves;
     Spreads out a wild strange sky where towering shapes,
50   Black and chaotic, choke the sickening day.
     Voices moan round; and from the sodden clay
     Mist-shrouds crawl up, in token that there gapes
     A grave for me at hand.   Aching with fears,
     I stumble towards the town, whose distant lights
55   Glint feebly and go out, and glint again,
     Like some retreating ship's unto the ken
     Of a lost man, who, sinking, feebly fights
     Alone in the wide waste behind.   The murmuring tone
     Of busy streets a moment gladdens me;
60   But there, too, comes the Spirit secretly;
     At feasts I see her shade, and am alone
     With thoughts of pain and nothing hear but her.

     So that I may not handle a keen knife,
     But flashes to the mind a fearful use
65   That men have made of it, to loose
     The heavy-weighted burden of their life
     And make an end. But Death is not the end:
     No death for such as thou, O Chatterton!
     Until the Second Death; and I do shun

70   The thought that death is misery's friend.
     Since my dread Ghost has once a finger laid
     Upon my flesh, and left a burning mark;
     This mark (saith she) shall fester on, and cark
     Till Death draw near, and halting, shade
75   His withering eyes, and know the Sign.
                                        O dense
     The darkness that shall flood around me then;
     Denser the clouds of biting arrows, when
     Vile devil-broods to torments bear me hence!

Written between September 1911 and May 1912.

TITLE   Cp. Tennyson, 'Supposed Confessions of a Second-Rate Sensitive Mind', and Coleridge, 'Dejection: An Ode'.
  8   southern strand: WO is referring to Keats's arrival in Italy in 1820.
 20   Perseus: The son of Danaë and Zeus, in Greek mythology. Polydectes, king of Seriphos, wishing to get rid of Perseus, sent him to fetch the head of the Medusa, one of the three Gorgons whose eyes turned men to stone. But Pluto lent Perseus a helmet that would make him invisible, Athene a shield (in which to see the Gorgons' reflection), and Hermes wings for his feet. He was thus able to escape the Gorgons' eyes and cut off the Medusa's head. WO returned to this theme in No. 82, 'Perseus' (p. 464).
63–7   Cp. *Hamlet*, III. i. 74–5: 'he himself might his quietus make / With a bare bodkin.'
67–8   Cp. Keats, 'To Chatterton', ll. 7–10:
                        Thou didst die
           A half-blown flow'ret which cold blasts amate.
           But this is past: thou art among the stars
           Of highest Heaven . . .

MSS, p. 200

18   O believe that God gives you
        All that he promises,
   A Saviour who forgives you,
        A perfect Saviour,
5   A Saviour full of power
      On the earth and in the heavens,
   A Saviour whose presence
       Alone makes happy.

      This Saviour will make you live
10   As he has lived.
   You will be able to follow him everywhere
       Without being conquered.
   Right to the end, in the conflict,
     His arm will protect you
15   And in the dark valley
       He will lead you.

This Evangelical chorus was written at Dunsden in May 1912.

MSS, p. 201

LITTLE CLAUS AND BIG CLAUS

There dwelled within a village, once, two men,
Whose names alike were Claus. Four stalwart mares
Had one; the other but a single nag.
Wherefore the richer wight *Big Claus* was called,
While men, if e'er they stayed to speak of him,
Would style his neighbour *Little Claus.* Now hark,
And you shall hear how fared it with them both,
For some do say my story is the truth.

All week, poor little Claus would plough for Big,
Lending his only horse; and then, in turn,
Big Claus would help one day in seven, with all
His team at work. Oh, proudly Little Claus
Curled the lithe whip over the horses five
On Sundays. Were they not as his, that day?
And, when the morning sun was warm, and mist
Rose from fresh furrows like the horses' steam,
While bells out-clamoured hungrily for folk
To fill the void and cavernous church, his heart
Would swell with pride to see the passers-by
Watching his labour; and he smacked his whip
And cried out 'Gee ho, my five horses.' 'Nay,'
Quoth Big Claus. 'That ye must not say, for one
Alone is thine.' Alas, no sooner came
Another well-clad churchman by, than Claus
Forgot the prohibition and its giver,
Forgot to guide the ploughshare even, and sang,
Not to the team but to the onlooker,
'Gee ho! my five horses!'
                        'Say it again,'
Growled Big Claus, menacing, and nodding slow
His head, much like the toiling nag itself,
'And I will knock thy beast upon the pate,
And make an end of it.' Then Little Claus
Ploughed on in silence; till a company
Of pleasant friends crossed o'er the fields, and called
Good-morrow to the tiller at his toil.
Pride set his thoughtless face once more aflush;

Full grandly he replied, and as they passed,
Briskly he clacked his whip. 'Gee ho!' he sang.
'Gee ho! my five horses.' Not a word
40 Spoke Big Claus, but he snatched a hammer up
And smote the hapless creature sudden-dead.
Oh, pitifully Little Claus did weep
To see his one horse dead, and reck his loss.
But afterwards he stripped away the hide
45 And dried it, till it stiffened in the wind;
Then packed it, slung the bag upon his back
And set foot to a neighbouring town to sell.
The afternoon o'ertook him on his way,
And with it, curdling storm clouds. 'Mid deep brakes
50 The tempest trapped him; and he wandered wide
Below dark sky and darker woods. At length
Firm shadows and a bar of yellow light,
Shining atop of shutters, beckoned him
Towards a farm. His knocking brought the Wife
55 To door; but 'No!' said she, an unknown man
She could not lodge, the Farmer being from home.
Claus turned round slowly from the sharp-slammed door,
And crept upon a thatch-roofed shed close by;
Whence, as he lay, and twisted him about,
60 He saw, above the scanty shutters, full
Into the kitchen; saw a table spread
With meats and fish and wine; and one there sat –
A Sexton – plying merrily his fork,
The whiles the Woman kept his glass abrim.
65 Claus watched, lamenting loud, and scarcely heard
The clatter of a heavy horse below.
This, the Farmer's horse, returning. He
Was a worthy man, but long he nursed
A curious prejudice against all Sextons,
70 Till the bare sight of one would make him mad.
So therefore did the Wife regale this one,
The Farmer absent; therefore, too, she now,
At his return, hustled the graveyard-man
Into an empty chest, and thrust the meats
75 Into the oven, the wines behind the stove.
'Alack,' moaned Little Claus, when all the feast

So vanished. 'Who's above?' the Farmer cried.
'Why liest thou there? Come, rather, in with me.'
Then Claus begged leave to spend the night with him.
80 'Yea, that thou shalt do; but we first must eat,'
Said he; and blithely 'gan to sup a dish
Of gruel, which the Woman set before them.
But Claus still hungered tigerishly for all
Those gravied savories; and relished ill
85 The milky groats. So now he placed his foot
Upon his bag, which lay beneath the board;
Making it squeak; and when it squeaked, said 'Hush!'
But saying so, trod harder, and called forth
Still louder noise. 'Hulloa!' said his host.
90 'What hast thou, in thy bag?'
                              'A wizard dwells
In this my bag,' said Claus; 'and wot ye now
What he is saying? Why that we should not
Be spooning gruel, when he's conjured up
Roast meat and pastries hot, inside thy oven there.'
95 'Zounds!' said the Farmer, peering in the stove.
Mutely the Woman drew her cooking forth
And so they ate. Again the enchanter spoke
In voice of chirping leather; telling now
Of three full wine jars, conjured by the stove.
100 Tongue-tied and fidgeting, the Wife fetched out
Her hidden bottles; so, the Farmer drank,
And was right merry. Presently, he said,
'And can thy mage bring up the Evil One?
I have a mind to see the Infernal sight,
105 Being in merry mood.' 'He can!' quoth Claus.
'Listen; he answers "Yes"; and he should do't
Only the sight is passing ugly.' 'Pooh!
I have no fear. What form, though, would he take?'
'Oh, he would have the image of a Sexton.'
110 'Nay, that's ugly indeed; for you must know
I cannot tolerate a Sexton. Still,
As I shall know it is the Evil One
The sight will be much easier to be borne.
Proceed, I'm ready; only – not too near!'
115 They sat awhile in silence, while the bag

Gave forth strange sounds. These Claus interpreted
As meaning that the Demon might be found
Cowering inside the oaken chest, all fear.
Full cautiously they stepped towards the thing;
120 Slowly and slightly raised they up the lid.
The Farmer peeped with eyes half-closed for dread,
Suddenly saw the quaking man, and sprang
Stammering away. 'Oh! Now, I've seen him. Ugh!
Exactly like our Sexton – shocking sight!'
125 So thereupon he needs must drink again,
And on they drank, till night was far advanced.
But when dawn brake, the Farmer rose and said,
'See, you must sell to me your Conjuror.'
'I cannot, – nay – I cannot; only think
130 Of all the benefit he is to me.'
Long Claus held out against entreaty thus;
Until, as if quick-touched with gratitude
To a kindly host, he parted with his bag
For a bushelful of money, measured fair.
135 'Moreover,' said the host, 'have thou the Chest;
'Who knows what ill may lurk within it yet?'
And bade the traveller, being well pleased withal,
Take a large barrow for removing it.
'Farewell!' quoth Claus, and pushed forth on his way.
140 A broad, but bridge-spanned river rolled athwart
The forest road; and when Claus gained the bridge
He stopped, hard breathing, questioning thus aloud:
'What if I rid me of this lurdane chest?
Heavy it is as it were filled with stone.
145 I'll trundle it no more. Belike the flood
Will bear it home; if not – then I care not.'
With that, he dragged and tilted it about
As if to heave it o'er the waterside.
'Hi!' shrieked the Sexton. 'Hi! man, leave it be!
150 Let me out first!' 'Ha! Zooks!' quoth Little Claus,
Feigning a fright. 'And is he still inside?
I'll haste and fling him in, so he may drown.'
'Oh no! No! No! A bushel of my wealth
Shall be your own, an you will set me free!'
155 At once the frolic knave undid the lock;

And out the Sexton crept, on crampèd knees.
Then, after gladly throwing the empty chest
Over the bridge, led Claus back to his house,
Meted the dole, and sent him home behind
160 A barrow now nigh full of shining coin.
To be assured of perfect measure, Claus
Dispatched a lad to Big Claus, craving for
The use of his best bushel. He, brain-teased
To know the cause of such a need, smeared tar
165 Upon the bottom of the vase; and lo!
The thing, returned, bore three new shillings, fast
Against the tar, bright moons in ebon sky.
Whence comes all this? thought he; and running straight
To Little Claus, was told it was the price
170 Of his dead horse's skin. 'A goodly price!'
Quoth he; and hastened home and smote his team
All dead; and hurried with their skins to town,
To make a mighty bargain. 'Who'll buy skins!'
He cried through all the streets; 'Skins! Skins!'
175 So brought the cobblers and the tanners out;
But they, being answered that his charge for each
Was a bushelful of money, thought he mocked,
And mocked again; until his senseless cries
Chafed them to wrath. 'Thou crazy loon!' yelled they,
180 'Thinkest we measure coin in bushels? Fie!
I'll warrant that we tan *thy* skin for thee
To colours black and blue'; and that they did,
With stirrups, belts and thongs and apron-bands.
So flailed him home, skin-seared with murderous stripes,
185 And burning hot with murderous thoughts within.
'The Knave shall pay for this; shall pay for this;
I'll kill him for his pains.' And, sure, that night,
He crept round to the house of Little Claus,
Stole to his bed, tho' scarcely seeing aught,
190 And struck the still, prone figure, dastardly
With pointed hatchet on the head; and left.
'The wicked man!' chirped Little Claus's voice
From out a corner. 'Tried to kill me! Oh!
Lucky for my grandame she was dead.'
195 For Little Claus's grandmother had died

That eve; and he, albeit her rancid tongue
Had vexed him oft, out-laid her in his bed,
Hoping the warmth might charm her life-warmth back.
He in a large chair dozed. From which he watched
200 Big Claus's deed. But soon as Claus was gone,
He dressed the dame in holiday attire,
Placed her upon the back seat of his cart,
And drove her, with a borrowed horse, towards town.
By sunrise, they had stopped outside an inn,
205 Whereof the landlord was a wealthy man,
And good; only as passionate as if
Composed of snuff and pepper. Of this man
Claus asked refreshment; answ'ring to his greeting,
'Yea, host, I stir betimes today; for I
210 Am taking my old grandame to the town.
She's in the cart: I cannot bring her in.
Perhaps, mine host, ye'll take her a glass of mead?
Speak loud; she's somewhat hard of hearing'.... 'Hem!'
The landlord cried, at the beldame's side,
215 Who sat up in the cart as if alive,
'Here is a glass of mead from your grandson, dame.'
Bolt upright sat the dame, nor moved an inch.
'Here is a glass of mead from your grandson, dame!'
Stark stared the dame, nor uttered she a word.
220 'Do ye not hear? Receive this glass of mead!'
Then, when he'd bawled the same a few times more,
As she ne'er stirred, he flew into a rage,
And flung the beaker full across her face.
At once she fell stiff backward to the ground.
225 'Hullo!' cried Little Claus, now rushing out,
And seizing on the landlord. 'What is this?
You've killed my grandmother! D'ye see this hole
Deep in her forehead?' 'Miserable me!
What a misfortune here! And all this comes
230 Of my too hasty temper!' Loud he moaned,
Wringing his hands. Then, 'Little Claus,' he said,
'Dear Little Claus, I'll have thy grandmother
Buried as if she were mine own; and you –
Shall have a bushel of my money, if
235 You speak no word of what has happened here.

For were it known, my head were not my own.'
So Little Claus took home another load
Of money, and the host inearthed the dame.

A second time, a lad rapped Big Claus' door,
240 Praying him lend a bushel to his friend.
In wide astonishment, he took the thing
Himself to Little Claus; who, smiling, said,
'You killed my grandmother instead of me!
I sold her for this bushelful of coin!'
245 Not long the elder stayed on hearing this;
But posted home to where his own shrunk gammer
Ever a-knitting sat, and ruthlessly
He struck her feeble spark of life extinct,
Like one that strikes with sudden iron the coals
250 And makes the low flame vanish into air.
This done, he drove to an apothecary
Off'ring to sell to him a defunct corse.
'Whose is it? And how came you by the same?'
'My grandmother's; I struck her dead to get
255 A bushel of thy money in exchange.'
'Lord help us!' said the man. 'Thou'rt surely mad!
If not, I vow your head's in jeopardy!'
And then he pointed out the heinousness
Of such a deed; the awful wickedness,
260 And punishment thereof; all which so scared
Big Claus, that, like a hounded hare,
He bolted from the shop, leapt on his cart,
And lashed his horses to a maniac's pace.
But maniac all thought the man; and so
265 They let him go wherever he might please.
Now, after reaching home, he knew one place,
One house, from which no man could turn his step
And that was Little Claus's.... When he stood
Facing that small deceiver, suddenly
270 He cast a roomy bag o'er all his length,
Tied it; and had him safe. He took his fill
Of wordy taunts and vaunts and promises
Of speedy drowning. Then to riverwards
He bore his prey to wreak the act itself.

275 None of the lightest was his cumbrous load;
     Long, very long his way; and, passing by
     A Church whence organ-tones were pealing forth,
     Big Claus bethought him he would rest therein,
     And hear a psalm before he further trudged.
280 Meantime, because he knew the strings were strong,
     And thought the people must be all in Church,
     He left the bag outside the open door.
     'Heigh-ho!' sighed Little Claus, a-squirming round
     And thrusting out his prison-sides, as if
285 Some monstrous ferret poked about its sack.
     But never a cord could he unloose; so lay
     Quite still again and thought. Ere long a herd
     Of cows came pattering by upon the dust;
     And when the pattering passed, he heard the slow
290 Tap-tapping of an ancient drover's staff.
     'Heigh-ho!' sighed Little Claus. 'I'm very young
     To be already bound for heavenly lands.'
     'And I,' the answer came, 'who am so old,
     Have never found the way to reach them yet.'
295 'Open the bag; creep in, instead of me,
     And thou shalt go to heaven in a trice.'
     'Then take my cattle, friend, and feed them well,'
     Said he; and Claus soon closed the bag o'er him
     And off he drove his thirty lusty cows.
300 The dust had scarcely settled in their rear,
     When Big Claus stepped into the sun again,
     And took his bag. 'How light it seems,' thought he.
     'That comes of hearing holy psalms, I ween!'
     So, easily he reached the river's banks,
305 And flung the bag a-gurgling to the deep.
     'There lie! I'll smart from no more tricks of thine.'
     But, walking home, at the forking of the roads,
     Who should he meet but Little Claus himself,
     Yelping at stubborn cattle. 'Mercy me!
310 How's this! Did I not drown thee!' gasped Big Claus.
     'Oh aye!' said he, as he thwacked a backward beast,
     'Oh aye! You threw me in the river there,
     Some half an hour ago.' Big Claus was dumb,
     And followed lamely on behind the herd.

| | At length he spoke: 'Where got ye all these kine?'
315 |
| | Said Little Claus: 'Sea-cattle is this herd.
| | I'll tell thee all the story; thanking thee
| | For having drowned me; since, escaping thus,
| | I'm very wealthy. Fearful was the fall
320 | Into the waters; down I sank at once,
| | But lighted on a bed of softest grass.
| | A moment afterward, the bag was loosed;
| | The loveliest girl imaginable, dressed
| | In snowy robes, and wreathed with dripping green,
325 | Gave me her gentle hand, and said, "O Claus,
| | There is some cattle for thee; if thou go
| | A mile along the Road, another herd
| | Thou'lt find; go, take it; as a gift from me."
| | I now perceived the river is a Road –
330 | The sea-folk's high road; there they walked and drove,
| | Passing from ocean far into the land.
| | How beautiful it was! How fresh the grass!
| | The fishes darted past my ear like birds,
| | And Oh the cattle grazing on the dikes!'
335 | 'Hum,' the other said. 'I marvel much
| | That ye return so soon from such a place.'
| | 'Why! 'tis a piece of policy, my friend!
| | I cross the fields towards my promised herd,
| | Because the River Road winds round about;
340 | And so I save much time.' . . . 'Thou lucky man!
| | Could I obtain sea-cows as thou hast done?'
| | 'No doubt thou could'st! If thou but walk with me,
| | Towards the banks, then get inside the bag,
| | I'd throw thee in with all the pleasure in life!'
345 | 'Thanks!' said Big Claus. 'But if I get no cows,
| | I'll beat you famously when I return.'
| | 'Nay, do not be so hard!' And so they went.
| | Now, as the drove of thirsty cows caught sight
| | Of running water, on they lumbered fast
350 | Towards it, tossing horns and lowing loud.
| | 'Look, look!' cried Little Claus. 'What haste they show!
| | How they do long to be below again!'
| | No sooner saw Big Claus that sudden rush
| | Than furious he waxed to be cast in.

355 'Give me a stone, for fear I should not sink!'
     He cried. 'No fear of that,' the other said.
     Still, in the bag he put a stone. Then pushed,
     And, plump! into the river fell Big Claus.
     'I fear he will not find the cattle, though,'
360 Said Little Claus. And away he drove his own.

Written at Dunsden in May 1912 (WO, 74). WO told SO on 15 May: 'I have finished a story from Anderson in Blank Verse; But I am dissatisfied with not only my attempt, but the story itself, which doesn't exactly inculcate peace and happiness, truth and justice, religion and piety' (CL, 136). This retelling of Anderson's tale closely follows the text of WO's own copy of *Little Klaus and Big Klaus* (illustrated by Chas. Pears, London and Glasgow: Gowans & Gray Ltd., 1906) except in one important respect: WO has consistently archaized his narrative.

    143 lurdane: worthless.

MSS, p. 202

THE RIVALS

    If thou guessed what easy hours
    I can fleet among my flowers,
    How I fondle them, and how
    Find them better friends than Thou,
5   Haply, love, the thing might shame thee;
    Haply with some spite inflame thee.

    Nay, indeed, thou art not all;
    And I can forget thy thrall.
    For I shall when summer comes
10 Sport me with my garden chums,
    Orchid, harebell, fern, and foxglove.
    Then thou'lt tear thy pretty locks, love,
    Twisting curls round jealous fingers. . . .

    When thou find'st thy true love lingers
15 Longer o'er the rose than thee,
    Know thou hast great rivalry;
    Cry to see it, careless elf,
    Bite thy lips, but blame thyself!

    Many a slim tree, dark of tresses,
20 Whispering, gives me strange caresses.
    Steadfast shines Narcissus' eye
    When I would his beauty try.
    And he loads my sighs with scent,
    Not with frowns of discontent.
25 Water lilies all tranquil lie
    When their secrecies I spy.
    Ruddy pout the mouths of roses –
    More I kiss, more each uncloses.
    Even violets, who are shy
30 Of their cousin in the sky,
    Do not stiffen or resent
    When a fingertip is bent
    Round their chins. And if, like thee,
    Little snowdrops were foot-free,
35 Would they run from me, and vent

          Laughs of scornful merriment?
          Nay, they love me, as I them.

          Oh, my loves of bud and stem,
          Tell my Maid what lightsome hours
    40   I spend with you in your bowers.
          This may pique her jealousy;
          Haply charm her back to me.

          Probably composed at Dunsden in 1912. The one MS is dated '1910 Dunsden'
          but, since this is a fair copy made at Bordeaux between June and August 1915, it
          seems likely that WO had forgotten he did not move into Dunsden vicarage
          until October 1911. On several occasions before that date he had stayed with the
          Gunstons at Kidmore End, and from there bicycled over to Dunsden with his
          cousins, but it is unlikely that 'The Rivals' was written before 1912.

          MSS, p. 203

A RHYMED EPISTLE TO E.L.G.
Mahim, Monkmoor Rd., in Salop

> 'Heigh ho! Howe dothe old Tyme gallop.'
> Bacon, *Promus*

Stanza 1

My honoured cousin,
              I'll not dwell
Longtime upon your verse (so *well*
Conceived) yet I am bound to tell
How after many a patient puff,
And later, many an angry snuff,
I got into a regular huff
    That you had never written
    To say how badly bitten
        You were by your exam,
    Or else how well you'd smitten
    The Oxford-Senior Witan
        By letting off your cram.

However . . .
So clever,
So well selected,
And so unexpected
Was this your happy rime
    It makes amend
For lapse of time,
    So here I end,
My chiding chime.

Canto II

> ... 'Is it physical
> To walk unbraced, and suck up the humours
> Of the dank morning?'
> *Cool-as a Cheeser*, Bacon

I will no more than mention
The Keswick grand convention
Such speech would be amiss
25 In such a thing as this.

What I can best remember
Of Keswick was the Camp
Pitched in a field as damp
As gutters in December.

30 We woke at six or thereabouts;
We woke to find our inner clouts
    As moist as Caustic Soda;
To find our tent, a *bell*-tent,
A very *bell-jar*, feculent
35 With CO₂, Cl, strong-blent
    With every pungent odour.

We lay at night between wet rugs
Found nothing, though, that rhymed with rugs –
And were the rugs a bit less hairy,
40 And were the tent a bit more airy,
Had fewer been the chilly gouts
That dropped upon our snoring snouts,
And warmer been the morning blast,
And daintier been the plain repast,
45 Less like strong bilge the stuff called tea,
Less like roast wood the pie-pastry
More plentiful the fruit and berry
– I wis we had bin very merry.

Canto III

> 'Hail!' Bacon's *Midsummer Iced Cream*
> Act III, scene i

I went to Coniston one day
50 And twice got drenched and had to pay
Hotels to dry the wet away.
The hail hailed, pricked and pained;
The rain rained, rained, and rained;
The clouds clouded, crowded round;
55 The thunder thundered; the wind – wound.

Canto IV

1 'Awake.'   Isaiah.
2 'Come forth.'   Bacon, *King John*, Act IV, sc. i.
3 'Come, prepare yourself'   do.
4 'See'st thou yon littel birde?'   Chaucer.
5 'Thank you.'   Christopher Marlowe.

All such as dwelled in the tent of *Sh! Hem!*
Now none of that! I mean – all them
As cohabit my canvas limpet
Were photographed thereby; and some imp hit
60 On th' idea of appearing in nightclo'es
(As the photographer came before 8 a.m.)
So in turbans of towels, and baggy pyjamas
We were actually taken; and what with the right-pose,
Right-*ex*posure, et cetera, we look like real 'salaamers'.

Canto v

> 'Damn all thieves'
> Keats

65 I can see how you stare
     At this startling quotation,
  Quite amazed that I dare
     Say that Keats thus could swear.
     But 'tis a citation
70   From one of his letters,
     And I make no filtration
     Of words of my betters;
       So there!

  And indeed I would add
75   'Secret Borrowers too',
  And every vile cad
     To whose mind 'me and you'
     Are one and the same.
  For I think it a shame
80 That my bike, so well prized,
  Some knaves have bestridden,
  And one has so ridden
     As to hug a stone wall
     Or somehow to fall,
85 And has made a nice mess,
  (Shape of pedal – an S)
  Hurt the mudguard no less
     And the nickel and all!

Epilogue

> *'Wind up.'*
> Bacon, *King Lear*, Act IV, sc. vii

I tried *in an hour*
90 To concoct this epistle;
– 'Twas beyond my poor power,
And, by that deep Whistle,
    I've been nearly two.
Time, then, for dismissal
95   And closing adieu.

Dear fellow, do send me
    Another of yours
For I've none to befriend me
    When Dunsden immures.

100 And perhaps I will send you
    Another of mine.

And so I commend you
    To heaven benign.

Written at Shrewsbury on 7 August 1912, this verse letter to ELG gives an account of WO's visit the previous month to an Evangelical Summer Convention at Keswick (WO, 76–7).

EPIGRAPH Bacon, *Promus*: Cp. WO to SO, 5 July 1912: 'I did some good work for Bacon, (as Shakespere.) Fine, if I can infect the College, eh?' (CL, 149). '*Promus*' is a facetious variation on *Comus*, like the variations on *Julius Caesar* and *A Midsummer Night's Dream* to which the epigraphs to Cantos II and III are ascribed.

STANZA I Evidently a mistake for 'Canto I'.

  11 Witan: council. ELG had recently sat the Oxford entrance exam.
  12 cram: knowledge that had been 'crammed'.
  35 CO_2, Cl: carbon dioxide, chlorine.
  49 Coniston: Visited probably as the childhood home of William Wordsworth. Cp. WO to SO, 21 July 1912: 'You will observe I have not a word to say about mountains or lakes or streams – Surely if Wordswth., Coleridge, Southey, Shelley, and Ruskin made it a matter of years to describe them, I cannot do so now, in this flapping, windy pavilion.' (CL, 150)
  58 canvas limpet: A bell tent has the shape of a limpet.

MSS, p. 204

25 THE DREAD OF FALLING INTO NAUGHT

Now slows the beat of Summer's dancing pulse;
Her voice has weak and quaverous undertones;
Cold agues in her hectic limbs convulse;
Slow palsies creep into her sapless bones.
5   Ah! is she falling into Death so soon, so soon?

Ev'n so! and now the peerless forest green
Is streaked with silvery pallor of decay.
As a beauteous woman's locks may lose their sheen
Through fearful dreams, and turn too early grey,
10 So Summer paleth now, and moaneth in her swoon.

The expressions of her once-rich mind, the flowers,
Are feeble-born, else rank unnaturally;
And whoso looks on leafy garden bowers,
Fresh bloodstains every misty morn may see,
15 Spilt from her veins by Winter's lance, and conflict-strewn.

My power of life, though youthful, also sinks;
Before my time I bear a hoary head;
And chill airs strike my brow, that blow, methinks,
Straight from the icy cavern of the dead.
20 Night darkens round; my day shall know no afternoon.

O never mourn, my brothers! well ye know
These crimson stains shall vanish from the trees;
Washed by the precious ointment of the snow.
A little while, and drowsy Earth's disease,
25 Shall feel the healing quickness of another June.

I, only, mourn, because I cannot tell
What spring-renewing wakes the sleep of Men.
I do but know, (ah! this I know too well)
I shall not see the same sweet life again,
30 Nor the dear Sun, nor stars, nor tender moon.

Written at Dunsden on 18 September 1912, according to the dated MS.

> 17   hoary head: Cp. Keats, *Endymion*, III. 218: 'The old man rais'd his hoary head.'

MSS, p. 204

34

Science has looked, and sees no life but this:
Or, at the most 'tis hypothetical.
'Thou art as animals, as worms, as clay;
Earth – thy small planet, of a thousand, one –
5 Shall slowly waste, unto an outburnt ash:
And thou and all thy race, be blotted out.
For in the dissolution of man's brain
Himself dissolves, and passes into naught' . . .

O careful Science, thou had'st all my zeal,
10 But a Third Power smiles, and beckons me.
She is a wanton of too light a name
To hold the faith of most men in her heart.
Poor Poesy! She hath no constancy . . .

But yesterday she clung half-trustingly
15 To calm religion. Where is she today?
Clasping Cold Science with a grim embrace!
No constancy! But comforts manifold,
And therefore, lovely to a waif, like me!

Speak to me, Poesy! Give me on this height
20 The one true message of thy thousand oracles!

'Yea? cryest thou so hungry for some Light?
Seek light no more! There is no Light as yet!
The Light that lights the soul shall be the last
Created thing; as that which lights the eye the first!
25 These mountains are the breasts of Mother Earth,
Nestle thou there, child; suck thy fill of joys.
And strive no more to look beyond thy Mother's arms.'

– So? is it so? Then I will lie and rest.
O mountains, there comes over me this hour
30 A wondrous longing for my latest sleep.
I long to drowse, and fall upon eternal sleep;
I want to sleep, but not to dream, and not to wake;
Pass hence, and yet behold no region more;
Fade from this company of distracted men
35 Where all are mad deluders, or else sick deluded . . .

Now, Night, rise softly like a careful nurse:
Lower the lights of day round thy sick child:
For I would sleep . . .
Poor I, who know not what I am, nor whence,
40   Would shake away this bitter case of flesh,
Even though naught remain when it is gone.
Would rid me of long deceiving blood;
How know I but at this very hour
My thoughts most high, most melancholy-grand,
45   Be not the chance-distemper of my pulse,
The doing of some small, intestine flaw!
O death, before I pluck my brain away,
Let me but sleep . . .
                      My heart stops – it is well . . .
50   O Light, which art but darkness,
O cruel world . . . O Men . . . O my own Self . . .
Farewell!

Written at Dunsden between September and November 1912.

    19–20 Cp. No. 1, 'To Poesy' (p. 3), and Keats, 'The Fall of Hyperion', l. 147: 'None can usurp this height.'

    31–2 Cp. *Hamlet*, III. i. 64–5: 'To die; to sleep – /To sleep? Perchance to dream! Ay, there's the rub.'

    40 Cp. *Hamlet*, I. ii. 129: 'O that this too too solid flesh would melt'; and *Antony and Cleopatra*, IV. xiv. 41: 'Crack thy frail case!'

    48 Cp. No. 148, 'Strange Meeting' (p. 149), l. 44: 'Let us sleep now. . . .'

MSS, p. 204

THE LITTLE MERMAID
of Hans Christian Anderson

Part 1

1

Far out at sea, the water is as blue
As cornflowers, and as clear as crystal-core;
But so exceeding deep, no sea-bird's view
Can fathom it, nor men's ropes touch its floor.
5   Strange, snake-like trees and weeds – the same which grew
Before dry land with herbs was peopled o'er –
Still sleep in heavy peacefulness down there,
And hold their fluctuous arms towards upper air.

2

And it is there the Sea-King's nation dwells.
10 His palace, golden-bright and ruby-red,
Gleams like a crown among those velvet dells.
Pink, shimmering streams of light its windows shed,
Like waterfalls of wine; and pink-white shells,
Like Alpine snows, its lofty roof o'erspread;
15 Which close and open, close and open wide,
With every ebb and flowing of the tide.

3

Twice beauteous is the sight, for perfect pearls
Glimmer between the valvelets as they gape.
As when a butterfly shut wings unfurls,
20 And pollen-filmèd globes of dew escape,
So ope those shells, so shine those gems. The swirls
Of stirring currents stroke to smoothest shape
The sandy palace floors; or, like a breeze,
Suddenly fluster its mysterious trees.

4

25 The ancient King, of consort long bereft,
Unto his mother gave the queenly state;
And in her careful governance he left
His six fair daughters. Scarce could I relate

       The beauty of those six without a theft
30 Of honey-words from some song-potentate;
       And of the youngest's utter loveliness,
       I rest content to wake a wistful guess.

5

       Her skin is delicate and freshly clear
       As petals of wild rose; and in her eyes,
35 As in the stillness of an evening mere,
       All heaven's purple concentrated lies.
       But lo! what marvel to mankind is here:
       She has no feet, no knees! but mermaid-wise,
       A fish's tail, smooth-tapering from her waist,
40 Blue-scaled, and glistering, like silver chased.

6

       All day, these mermaids sported in their hall,
       Feeding the fish that through the windows shot,
       And training weeds to twine about the wall.
       Or sometimes each would tend her garden grot,
45 Where one so ranged her plants as to recall
       Blunt-snouted whales; another planned her plot
       In shapes to imitate her own; and one,
       The youngest, choosing red flowers, made a sun.

7

       A strange and lonely child seemed this Princess.
50 Deep were the fathomings of her secret thought.
       Not that she shunned a sisterly caress;
       But, spoken to, faint-smiled, and answered naught.
       Loved she the silent deep? Nay, less and less
       She loved it! And as years new sameness brought,
55 Its silence, its low stillness, its pale gloom,
       Weighed on her soul, and made sweet life a doom.

8

       Her sisters joyed to find such curious things
       As foundering ships let fall to their domain;
       But she cared not for showered coins or rings,
60 And claimed no share of all that precious rain

Except a marble statue, – some boy-king's,
Or youthful hero's. Its cold face in vain
She gazed at, kissed, and tried with sighs to thaw,
For still the wide eyes stared, and nothing saw.

9

65 Thereby she set a weeping-willow tree
To droop and mourn. Full dolefully it clung
About the form, and moved continually,
As if it sighed; as if it sometimes wrung
Convulsive fingers in sad reverie.
70 And ever o'er the light blue sand it hung
A purple shade, which hour by hour the same,
Burnt softly on, like lambent sulphur flame.

10

Soon, for the twilight of that shadow's ring,
The girl forsook the fiery-blossomed grove
75 And golden-fruited gardens of the King;
Yet not e'en there her eyes reposed; but strove
For glimpses of the sun's far brightening.
Her ear could bear no voice, unless it wove
Tales of the upper world; its tuneful birds;
80 Sweet-odoured blooms; warm meadows; placid herds.

11

Long time before these wonders might be seen
By her, for it was now the year wherein
The eldest sister counted years fifteen.
(Now sea-folk hold it as unthinkable sin
85 For girls to wander from their sire's demesne
Until a certain year of age they win.)
Rose the first Princess to the waves at last,
And there, in wonderment, a long night passed.

12

Returned, she told her sisters all; and said
90 Naught was so fine as, from a sandy isle,
To watch a city's lights, white, green, and red,
Pricking the dark for many a twinkling mile.

She caught strange music, and, more strange, the tread
   Of crowded men. Then, from some campanile,
95 Hummed the low voices of the midnight bells,
   And bugles fluted in far citadels.

   13
   A year went; and the second happy maid
   Broke the still surface of the evening sea.
   The sky was peerless gold; a slow parade
100 Of violet clouds wheeled westward gorgeously.
   Above her, like a white and fluttering braid,
   The wild swans winged towards the sun. Then she
   Swam westward too; but swift the great ball sank,
   Leaving the air all colourless and dank.

   14
105 The third Princess was bold: she made her way
   Far up a river, passing vine-clad hills,
   And wooded castles all the sunny day.
   Oft-times she had to dive or take cool swills
   To ease her burning skin. She fain would play
110 With bathing children; but with terror-shrills
   They fled from her; and when dogs barked amain,
   She too took fright, and turned to sea again.

   15
   The fourth remained in mid-seas; whence, said she,
   A vast blue bell of glass appeared the vault.
115 Dim sails she spied; and watched the tireless glee
   Of waggish dolphins turning somersault,
   And whales a-snorting fountains angrily.
   The fifth went up in winter, when like malt
   The surge was frothing, and the drifting ice
120 Shone green as emerald thrones of Paradise.

   16
   She took a slippery seat on one of these,
   And let the winds fan out her long, wet hair.
   The near ships scudded on before the breeze
   As if alarmed to see her. . . . Then the air

125   Fell vaporous-heavy; ocean, ill at ease,
        Belched spray; but safe upon her swinging chair,
        She laughed to see the vessels roll and leap,
        And lightnings zigzag o'er the seething deep.

        17
        It often happened that the sisters five
130   Would rise with arms entwined at twilight brown.
        O! it was sweet to see them upward drive
        Light as the clustered balls of thistledown.
        Then would they sing, and singing sometimes strive
        To tell storm-tossers not to fear to drown.
135   But men, who take their voices for the wind,
        Must perish ere they reach the sea-folk kind.

        18
        Said I those linkèd evening flights were sweet?
        Ah! not so unto one! . . . who stood and gazed
        Until the lightnings from the distant beat
140   Of lashing tails she saw no more; then raised
        Her eyes to where the large, pale stars did fleet
        Through gliding shadows, and so dreamed amazed
        Of shadowy ships; which guessed not the appeal
        Of mermaid arms outstretched towards their keel.

        Part II

        19
145   So dreamed she through the years; until, oh joy!
        The day of her ascension surely came.
        Now must the grandame tedious skill employ,
        In dressing her as should befit her name.
        Though truly all this pomp did but annoy
150   The Princess: often, with a hurt exclaim,
        She would have shaken off the eight large shells
        That decked her tail; and ev'n her asphodels.

        20
        But 'Pride must suffer pain' the dame averred,
        And wove the heavy wreath about her brow.

155 However, all forgotten at the word
'Farewell', she shot up lightsomely enow.
Many a silver bubble she bestirred
To quiver up as up she sped; and now,
Herself a bubble, burst upon the air,
160 And lost herself within its wonders rare.

21

The sun that moment dipped, but fairy pink
Still flushed the clouds, and long their trailing fringe
Swept on, and waved above the airy brink
Where day was slipping from the earth. A tinge
165 Curdled the sea, like mingling oil and ink,
Or bloody lymph when witch's flames impinge.
And in the midst of that wide calm, there lay
A large, dark ship, still as a rock, and grey.

22

Only one sail was hoist, for no breeze stirred.
170 The sailors all about the rigging hung
In easy pose, each like a dozing bird.
Soft music breathed at times, clear voices sung;
And when the shine of eve grew blurred,
Hundreds of lantern fires on high were slung.
175 Sudden, the dazzle of a rocket-glance!
And on the deck strikes up the merry dance.

23

The mermaid, close beneath, essays to peep
Through the transparent cabin panes; and oft
As she is lifted by the billow-leap,
180 Espies young human forms, more beauteous-soft
Than she had dreamed; but oh! she holds these cheap
Beside their Prince. Anon he goes aloft,
Whereat a hundred fireworks skyward hiss,
Fright'ning the maid far down the dark abyss.

24

185 When next she looks, the stars of heaven seem falling;
Suns drizzle sparks, and all is light as day.

So that amid the din and flash appalling,
　　　She clearly sees the glistening pleasure-ray
　　　Gleam from the Prince's eye, as he is calling
190　For songs, and smiling on his comrades gay.
　　　Why is his smile so sparkling and elate?
　　　Surely his birthday they must celebrate!

　　　　25
　　　See how the poesy trembles on his lip
　　　To hear the pining violins, heart torn,
195　Yearn to the lightsome harps, that o'er them trip,
　　　Like elves about Titania, love-lorn!
　　　Ah, hark, though – in the shrouds above the ship –
　　　How envious winds now bodefully 'gin mourn!
　　　The sighing of their wailful harmonies
200　Hath hushed the lutings and the chaunted glees.

　　　　26
　　　It is late. Starry lamps and fierce fusees
　　　Fade out. The stunning guns are dumb. All ears
　　　Hark to grumbling in the heart of the seas.
　　　The ship makes sudden headway; on she steers,
205　Her canvas spreading to the strengthening breeze;
　　　Till lightning shows a dark shore quickly nears.
　　　Whereat the mariners reef again the sails,
　　　And know they lie at mercy of the gales.

　　　　27
　　　The mermaid, clinging to the vessel's side,
210　Bounding from crest to crest with dizzy swoop,
　　　Fancies they run a right good billow-ride.
　　　The crew, all huddled on the drenching poop,
　　　Think differently. Fresh leaks split gaping-wide;
　　　A mountain-wave bursts o'er a shrieking group,
215　And sweeps them deep into the deep cold.
　　　The mast falls headlong; water fills the hold;

28

She heels slowly – leans – sinks – O Heaven – she sinks!
With gasp and bubbling groan the brave ship goes,
She and her braver souls. . . . The nymph but thinks
220   Of one; and him, just as his eyelids close,
Just as his mouth draws in the first death-drinks,
She finds, upholds, and guides between the floes
Of battling planks and spars of splintering wood.
Then lets the billows bear them where they should.

29

225   At dawn, the outspent wind sank down as dead;
And gloriously uprist the eastern hues.
They touched the Prince's pallid cheek with red,
And soon with certain life he did infuse.
The nereid kissed him; fondled his fine head,
230   And smoothed his hair so marred with clammy ooze.
He seemed her statue grown life-sensitive!
She kissed again, and knew that he would live.

30

Now they approached a balmy, sunlit land,
Whose marble mountains, silver-tipped with snow,
235   Towered o'er a seaboard fringe of citrons bland.
She swam to where a domèd portico
Crowned shallow waves; and, passing up the sand,
Laid down her sleeping burden there-below.
Then she drew back, and hid beneath thick foam,
240   To watch for whoso thitherward might roam.

31

Ere long there issued from that building white,
A crowd of straying girls. Soon one of these
Beheld the prostrate corse; half choked with fright,
She uttered cries; then, falling on her knees,
245   Besought him speak. He stared, smiled, rose upright.
And with those maidens vanished through the trees.
But no smile sent he to the watching one,
Nor knew he aught of all that she had done.

32

Stricken, as with a wound, she stiffly fell
250   Into her father's halls; and from that hour,
Her pensiveness increased tenfold. 'What spell',
They asked her, 'doth thy budding life deflower?
Show us this hidden woe. Thou wilt not tell?
Sister, what sights of ship, or cloud or tower,
255   Bewitched thee on thy happy day above?'
– Empty request! How dared she say 'twas Love!

33

Till, after lingering by that quiet beach,
Marking the dazzling snow-caps slowly melt,
Fruits ripen, cornfields mellow, pastures bleach,
260   And last, the acorn showers begin to pelt,
But seeing nevermore the Prince, her speech
Could hold no more: all, all she felt
And longed for, poured she out in piteous sobs.
And lo! in flooded Hope with glorious throbs!

34

265   For none among her kindred maids but burned
To help their sister's love, so destitute;
And 'twas not long ere one of them had learned
Where dwelt this Prince of high terrene repute.
So henceforth her fond spirit no more yearned
270   Unto a vision, once-seen, stark and mute,
But now she held him in her constant sight,
And stayed beneath his casement night by night.

35

He thought himself alone on many a night
While she was close; and gave no noteful heed,
275   When, in the shadows, murmured ripples slight.
Once, ev'n, as she was hid in bedded reed,
A gust seized hold her silvery veil so light.
But he who saw, must needs the rest instead,
By saying: 'Lo! a swan that spreads its wings!'
280   – How blind are men to twilight's mystic things!

Part III

36
Much looking and much brooding on the earth,
Desire unsated, daily growing worse,
Begot in her young brain the sudden birth
Of an idea – too strange for her to nurse.
285 Therefore with fervidness, though feigning mirth,
She brought it to the Queen: 'Sweet dame, rehearse
More and yet more of the world that's dry.
Bears it immortal lives? Or do men die?'

37
So she began, and thus the Queen replied:
290 'They die, my child, they die. And their life's term
Is shorter than our own. We here abide
Three hundred years; then, like the basest worm,
Dissolve into the foamy ocean-tide.
Now men have brief existence and infirm,
295 But after, they ascend beyond the stars,
Where tears are not, and naught their rapture mars.'

38
'And why have we no such undying soul?
Oh, I would give my mermaid centuries
For one day human, and Hope's aureole.'
300 'Think not of that; we of the underseas',
The lady said, 'live happier and more whole
Than men do, with their early grave, disease,
And void despairs. For not all hope as thou,
Nor is Life's crown for every human brow.'

39
305 'So, at the last, to empty surf I melt;
Drift on the gabbling waves, yet hear no word;
Froth in the soft, warm rains, that fall unfelt;
Fly before whistling winds that pipe unheard
And know no more the place where I have dwelt.'
310 'And better so! Why, 'less reports have erred,
Many a human life hath envied thine,
And thy long sleep upon the windy brine.'

40

'But is there no way whereby I might find
A spirit like to man's?' 'No way, dear girl,
Unless it chanced some rashling of their kind,
So loved you that you were to him a pearl,
More goodly than his own wide world enshrined,
And wedded you. Nay, mark! 'Twould be a churl
Who'd do it. This magnificent tail of yours
Offends their youth. Four limbs, else no men-wooers!

41

'Come, come, be merry! Let us leap about
During the span of years we have to live.
Thou'lt find it long enough, beyond a doubt,
To welcome Death, a blessèd lenitive.
Tonight we give a ball: attend this rout;
'Twill stir thy wits: thou'rt too contemplative.'
In radiant revelry soon came the mermen all
And nymphs, and staring fishes, great and small.

42

For ocean hummed with music through and through
And the shades were phosphor-sheened. 'Rejoice! Rejoice!'
The dancers sang; the Princess chanted too,
Delighted; and that night she knew her voice
To be the loveliest and most flawless-true
E'en heard on land or sea. Yet 'twas her choice
To steal away from all the vast applause,
Unto her garden, there from mirth to pause.

43

A bugle sounded through the far dark wave.
'Ah, now', she moaned, 'he surely sails aloft;
He for whose warm, celestial love I crave;
He who could give me in two kisses soft
All joy in life, and all beyond the grave.
Lo! I will venture all for him! What oft
I feared, tonight I'll face. What other help?'
Thereat she 'gan to wind through groves of kelp,

44

345 Towards the abysmal deserts, where the flood
Spins fierce in spiral phantasies; which, crossed,
Led to a region of warm, bubbling mud,
With slimy weeds and greenery bemossed,
And serpent-polypi, that feed on blood,
350 And hug old rust, gaunt hulks and treasures lost.
Between their ever-groping arms the lithe girl shot,
A shuddering lightning; then sank safe – on what?

45

– The witch's den! Around was filthy quag,
In whose soft mire slow-wallowed water slugs,
355 Large, fat, and white. There sat the fishy hag,
Beneath her hut of bones. About her dugs
Clung toads; while snakes, with lazy drag,
Wound round her arms, which she, with fulsome hugs,
Embraced and stroked, and fed from her own mouth.
360 This horror parched the maid's full voice like drouth.

46

'I know, I know why thou art come, fair fool!
Would'st rid thee of thy tail, and wear instead
Two props, according to the earth-folk's rule;
All this that some young prince may love and wed
365 Thy beauty. So, too, shall ye overrule
High fate, which orders that our dead keep dead,
Not live for aye, as men do fable. Bah!
Hoo-hoo! Buy legs to steal thee wings! Ha-ha!'

47

So loud and so repulsive laughed the witch,
370 The very reptiles fell upon the ground,
And there lay wriggling. Then 'I'm not so rich',
Quoth she, 'as to refuse a Princess crowned.
Have thy mad will. I'll charm a potion which,
Mark ye! shall give thee legs, straight, white, and sound,
375 But hurt it must as swords were probing ye.
Drink it at sunrise, sitting near the sea.

48

'All who behold thee in thy changèd state
Shall call thee fairest mortal, beauty's queen.
Thine agile, floating elegance of gait
380 Thou shalt retain; no dancer ever seen
May move so light as thou. But wait, child, wait!
Each step ye take will cost ye pain as keen
As if ye trod on knives. An ye do choose
To bear these pangs, my magic I will use.'

49

385 'I do,' replied the mermaid; but she shook
As shake the weeds below the surface-storm.
'Bethink ye well: thy fish-tail once forsook,
Ye cannot change again from human form,
Nor ever on thy father's Palace look.
390 And should ye find your Prince not quite so warm,
And fail to win his love – such love that he
Break from his old delights to cleave to thee –

50

'Thou diest: the soul thou reachest after, missed;
Life thrown away. The day he weds his choice
395 Shall be thy last. Ocean shall be thy cist;
His solemn breast, spurned for a fickle boy's,
Shall nurse thee; shrivelled into spumy mist!
And now, child, pay my dues. I want thy voice.
Needest its tones to charm him, little witch?
400 Nay, give thy best for this my ichor rich.'

51

'But if thou take my voice, what have I left?'
'Thy buoyancy! Thy matchless mould! Thine eyes!
Come! Let me cut thy tongue, nor think it theft.'
'Take it! . . . O Prince! . . . O sweet immortal prize!'
405 Pale as a faint moon in a stormy cleft
Was her drawn mouth, and wild as winds her sighs.
But from complaint she utterly forbore.
So yielded up her voice, and spake no more.

52

Forthwith the sorceress brought forth her pot,
And having scoured it well with knotted snakes,
Dripped in from her own veins black bloody clot;
Then added poisons, bones, and weird mandrakes;
So that there roamed around the cauldron hot,
Fumes such as rise when rousèd Etna quakes.
Whilst the loud simmering of that mystic chyle
Droned like the wailings of a crocodile.

53

These spells complete, the mermaid took the juice,
Which seemed as water from the purest fount,
Safe passed the polyps and the whirling sluice
(For the dread charm o'er these was paramount).
Then, hovering o'er her home, she strove to loose
Love's hindering thongs from round her heart. But 'Mount!'
A stronger Love was crying, 'Fast to shore!'
So, in great grief, she slowly 'gan to soar.

54

While yet the sapphire night bedomed the world,
Aground, and 'neath the palace water stair,
Waiting the charmèd dawn, she lay upcurled.
In swoon she lay, and she was unaware
How, after break of day, the wavelets purled
About her feet, and licked her ankles bare.
But so it was: the potion of the seer
Had worked its work, and heaven was very near.

Part IV

55

The pang that broke her sleep was quickly spent,
Quenched in a bliss, above all blisses sweet:
None other than the Prince above her bent!
Their earnest eyes like magnet-steels did meet.
She, dropping lids before his gaze intent,
First saw her marble shining limbs complete;
And joyed. But on the instant was amate,
For from her eyes no word could he translate.

56

Much wond'ring why so rich a mouth were mute,
He gently led her towards the stately door.
Even as she foreknew, stabbings acute
Tortured her tread; which willingly she bore,
445 Although she looked to see the blood out-shoot.
But no stain lay upon the yellow shore.
Only the ribbèd sand was soft and sodden,
Molten to jelly, where her soles had trodden.

57

Thus hand in hand with him her beauteous Prince,
450 Up the broad steps she flew, like wafted bubble.
– And never was she known to cry or wince,
For all the anguish of that secret trouble.
And then they dressed her, as before or since,
Few girls have been. For favour she had double
455 The other inmates of that courtly place.
And all the land made marvel at her face.

58

The Prince soon found a name to call her by:
Philotis; which was linked on many a lip
With his name, Philo, in a tone full sly.
460 Greatly he loved to watch her deft feet trip.
For slaves would frisk, and swim, and sprawl and fly,
But tiptoe Lotis almost seemed to slip
Into the air and float upon her arms.
So more the realm was ravished by her charms.

59

465 Those slaves would also sing, with mimic glee.
Ah, why should young Philotis fall so sad,
When Philo praised them? – 'Twas not jealousy!
But soon a heavier grief than this she had:
Though loved as any fair young child might be,
470 Though dear as many a lass to one same lad,
She was not the devotion of his life;
He never dreamed to take her as his wife.

60

Long, long she feared to think it; yet 'twas plain;
And every day the certainty increased.
By night, new thoughts would steal upon her brain
Wild as the far-off cry of some strange beast.
And Philo's sweetest laugh became her bane.
And though his merry kisses had not ceased,
She knew her mouth, that never might unclose,
Must seem a blighted bud, a scentless rose.

61

And thus she let her colour fade away,
And languished for cool waters, like a flower.
The more so when her sisters left their play
To watch continually beneath her tower,
And nightly sing how sore was their dismay.
Once, she perceived the King, for one short hour,
And once the agèd Queen; but not anear.
They had not risen so for many a year.

62

'My Lotis,' said Prince Philo, one soft eve,
'My parents wish me married, as you know,
And bid me see their choice; but had I leave,
I would not think of this same Princess. No!
I love not an unknown. I had as lieve
Wed thee, Philotis, as commit me so.
For thou resemblest one I love full well,
Who saved my life: a heavenly damosel.

63

'When I was wrecked, and cast on foreign shore,
She succoured me; she saved me from the sea.
Twice saw I her; I shall not see her more.
But something of her beauty lives in thee.
Forgive me if too ardently I pore
Upon thy face; kind fate has sent thee me,
And thou hast driven her image from my heart.
Kiss me, Philotis; we must never part.'

64

505 So when he sailed away in gallant state,
To meet the daughter of a neighbouring king,
Lotis went with him. Then to her he'd prate
Of calms and tempests; fishes; everything
The deep reveals where divers penetrate,
510 Supposing that she listened wondering.
And sooth she gazed into the waves full hard,
As if they were not dark to her regard.

65

Both day and night her lonely watch she kept,
Leaning above the milky, glistening foam;
515 Whiles all men save the silent helmsman slept,
And once she thought she saw her ancient home.
And every dusk her sisters rose and wept,
And almost to her side the five upclomb.
By signs she told them she was happy still,
520 Beloved of men; and nowise treated ill.

66

The ship reached port; and, in magnificence,
Prince Philo waited for his promised bride.
Days did he wait, in nervous indolence.
At last she came. The Prince's eyes flashed wide
525 With sudden ecstasy; in voice drawn tense
By all the mighty joy of years untried,
And played upon by stroke of present passion,
He chanted (while Philotis' lips grew ashen):

67

"Tis thou! 'Tis thou! Sans whom were I now dead!'
530 And for a while he could nor think nor say,
But even as her little curly head
Was shut between his shoulders quite away,
So in her being, his soul was burièd,
And hidden from the glare of common day.
535 She was indeed the damsel of the sands!
Well, well may poor Philotis wring her hands!

68

Why should I tell how fine the bridals were,
How many flaming heralds rode the streets,
Or what loud peals went rioting through the air,
Or how the towns were choked with wine and meats,
Since Lotis of these things was not aware?
Forlorn Philotis! Scalding chills and heats,
Visions wherein one face did ever melt,
And, with it, worlds, were all she saw and felt.

69

'Twas so, though still she danced as she was used,
Danced out and far beyond the reach of Art,
For she forgot her feet were sadly bruised.
Her Prince had said: 'You will rejoice, sweetheart,'
So she forgot her soles were sore contused,
Because the sharper pain was at her heart.
Thus the great wedding day came, blazed, and passed,
And fell the night which was to be her last.

70

It found her on his vessel, homeward bound.
Musicians, sailors, revellers, were withdrawn.
The sea was tranquil, heaving without sound.
Already, o'er the east, wan chasms yawn.
The passing billows, weltering mound on mound,
Shone ghastly in the doleful light of dawn.
Then saw she how five mermaids rose all pale,
To save her, if their plan might aught avail.

71

No more their lovely locks streamed out, wind-fanned.
'We gave them to the witch', they said, 'for this,'
And pressed a dagger in her loathful hand.
'Strike deeply at his heart: it cannot miss.
So shalt thou conquer Fate, and Death withstand.
For when his blood shall sprinkle thee, we wis,
Thy feet shall close into a tail once more.
Thus all may be as it hath been before.'

72

So, shrilling, 'Haste!' they sank. And night was spent.
Then she, approaching where the bridegroom slept,
Lifted the scarlet curtain of his tent.
The slumbering pair she saw, and to them crept.
So close they lay, their very curls were blent,
And both her hands beneath his cheek he kept.
Philotis, kneeling, stole her last embrace.
Then turned and watched the sky, a little space.

73

She scanned the coming colour breathlessly,
As 'twere some fateful cauldron, heaving slow.
And now the dull and heavy-clouded sky
Gave forth a steady and increasing glow,
As tarnished lead, that heat doth glorify,
A weird and ruddy brilliancy can throw.
Sudden, like bubble on hot metal seething,
Bulged the great sun. Then ceased Philotis' breathing.

74

Still stood she by the spoiler of her life,
List'ning his dreamy murmurs. What she caught
Was ever one same word: 'Fair wife, sweet wife.'
Ah, She, She only filled his heart and thought!
And Lotis' fingers clutched the raisèd knife.
But ere the fountain of his blood it sought,
It hurtled back, and splashed along the wave,
And she had leapt into the sea: her grave.

75

The sun passed flaming up his azure path,
And warmed the drift of froth that erst was flesh.
She felt the radiance, and as from a bath,
Uprist into the air, ethereal, fresh.
She had not feathers, as an angel hath,
Nor fairy wings of clear and gauzy mesh;
But yet slid upward, like a lifting mist,
And floated, cloudlike, though heaven's amethyst.

76

Around her, floated spirits fair as she.
No fear she felt of their so perfect form,
Nor of their tongues' angelic melody,
Nor of the numbers of that rosy swarm.
605 They told her of their office and degree:
To heal the pestilence; to still the storm;
To fan the atmosphere of fiery regions;
Guide honey-bees, and pilot swallow legions.

77

But what they whispered of her after-fate,
610 The years which this sweet work must see elapse,
Before her final, heavenly estate,
I have not learned. She worketh yet, perhaps;
This evening's sunset may illuminate;
Maybe your garden's tender buds she wraps;
615 Or breathed the scent into the rose you wear,
Or even now, is smiling by your chair.

78

No more than this knows he that told her tale:
That, looking through the vapours under her,
She saw the ocean, and one lonely sail.
620 On board was weeping and unwonted stir.
Both Philo and his bride were very pale.
She heard his hushed, half-sobbing voice aver:
'Woe! Woe! The child hath cast herself away!'
And kissed them, gazing on the pearly spray.

Written at Dunsden after WO had finished his blank-verse retelling of another of Hans Andersen's tales, 'Little Claus and Big Claus' (No. 19, p. 17) (WO, 78–80). On 17 September 1912, he wrote to SO: 'The other day I started afresh on *The Little Mermaid* and have done 19 stanzas. Would you like to hear one of the best?' He then quoted a version of stanza 9 (CL, 161). Later that month, he told HO: 'I have now written 30 stanzas of "The Little Mermaid" – and not half done yet' (CL, 74; Letter 82 is there misdated). The poem was probably completed that autumn.

29–30 Cp. Keats, *Endymion*, III. 426–7: 'With . . . honey-words she wove / A net.'
  91 Cp. No. 102, 'The city lights along the waterside' (p. 105).
 111 amain: greatly.
 114 Cp. Shelley, 'Adonais', l. 462: 'Life, like a dome of many-coloured glass'.
119–20 Cp. Coleridge, *Ancient Mariner*, ll. 53–4: 'And ice, mast-high, came floating by, / As green as emerald.'
 153 Cp. Coleridge, *Ancient Mariner*, l. 93: 'For all averred, I had killed the bird.'
164–6 Cp. Coleridge, *Ancient Mariner*, ll. 129–30: 'The water, like a witch's oils, / Burnt green, and blue and white.'
 196 Titania: Queen of the fairies. See *A Midsummer Night's Dream*.
 226 Cp. Coleridge, *Ancient Mariner*, ll. 97–8: 'Nor dim nor red, like God's own head, / The glorious Sun uprist.'
 230 Cp. Keats, 'Isabella', xxxv: 'the forest tomb / Had marred his glossy hair.'
356–9 Cp. Spenser, *Faerie Queene*, I. i. 15: 'Of her there bred / A thousand yong ones, which she dayly fed, / Sucking upon her poisonous dugs.'
 395 cist: sepulchral chamber.
 397 Cp. Keats, 'To Homer', l. 7: 'And Neptune made for thee a spumy tent.'
 415 chyle: digestive juices.
 439 amate: daunted.
 447 Cp. Coleridge, *Ancient Mariner*, l. 227: 'the ribbed sea-sand'.
 493 I had as lieve [lief]: I would as gladly.
 566 wis: know.

MSS, p. 205

32 THE TWO REFLECTIONS

I seldom look into thy brown eyes, child,
But I behold in them the deep, cool shade
Of summer woods. Hence always, if dismayed
To think how quickly Time hath us beguiled
5   Of those enchanted days, when forest-wild,
We roamed the copses, and so gaily played;
I feel about me yet the dusky glade,
And June's late light through long lanes, beechen-aisled.
And in the glistening of thy fragrant hair
10 Sparkles the scented rain that glistened then.
But ah! I see, too, thou being otherwhere,
Thy shadowy eyes in every low-lit glen;
Thy locks in every sun-gilt shower, and there
In those sweet glooms, find sorrow unaware.

Written probably in autumn 1912, this poem may be a recollection of the river trip described in WO's letter of 27 June 1912 to MO: 'For tea, we moored up against a beech-wooded escarpment, miles long, on the left bank. I and three élite, adventuresome children climbed to the top; and came down at a breathless rate. . . . We reached Caversham about 7.30; and I of course rode home; but I thought of two little feet that had to walk, even to beyond the Vicarage, and was troubled.' (CL, 145) The 'two little feet' were probably those of 'mine own favourite Milly [Montague]'.

MSS, p. 207

Deep under turfy grass and heavy clay
They laid her bruisèd body, and the child.
Poor victims of a swift mischance were they,
Adown Death's trapdoor suddenly beguiled.
5   I, weeping not, as others, but heart-wild,
Affirmed to Heaven that even Love's fierce flame
Must fail beneath the chill of this cold shame.

So I rebelled, scorning and mocking such
As had the ignorant callousness to wed
10 On altar steps long frozen by the touch
Of stretcher after stretcher of our dead.
Love's blindness is too terrible, I said;
I will go counsel men, and show what bin
The harvest of their homes is gathered in.

15 But as I spoke, came many children nigh,
Hurrying lightly o'er the village green;
Methought too lightly, for they came to spy
Into their playmate's bed terrene.
They clustered round; some wondered what might mean
20 Rich-odoured flowers so whelmed in fetid earth;
While some Death's riddle guessed ere that of Birth.

And there stood one Child with them, whose pale brows
Wore beauty like our mother Eve's; whom seeing,
I could not choose but undo all my vows,
25 And cry that it were well that human Being
And Birth and Death should be, just for the freeing
Of one such face from Chaos' murky womb,
For Hell's reprieve is worth not this one bloom.

Written at Dunsden between late October 1912 and June 1913. On 15 October 1912, WO had assisted at the double funeral of Alice Mary Allen and her four-year-old daughter, Hilda Agnes (WO, 80–1).

MSS, p. 208

35 Unto what pinnacles of desperate heights
   Do good men climb to seize their good!
   What abnegation to all mortal joys,
   What vast abstraction from the world is theirs!
5 O what insane abuses, desperate pangs,
   Annihilations of the Self, soul-suicides,
   They wreak upon themselves to purchase – GOD!
   A God to guide through these poor temporal days
   Their comings, goings, workings of the heart,
10 Obsess, indeed, their natures utterly;
   Meanwhile preparing, as in recompense,
   Mansions celestial for their timeless bliss.
   And to what end this Holiness; this God
   That arrogates their intellect and soul?
15 To none! Their offered lives are not so grand,
   So active, or so sweet as many a one's
   That is undedicate, being reason-swayed;
   And their sole mission is to drag, entice
   And push mankind to those same cloudy crags
20 Where they first breathed the madness-giving air
   That made them feel as angels, that are less than men.

Completed at Dunsden on 6 November 1912, according to the dated MS (WO, 81–2).

MSS, p. 209

IMPROMPTU

I have none other thought of peace, but only Thee.
  – By which I know thou art not of this world.

One time, the world contained great store of friends,
  Mother and Brethren, Teachers, Holy Guides,

5 All tender to my foolishness; all dear to me;
  But this last woe they would not understand.

I once had hopes of heaven, whereon I slept and smiled,
  But a cold hand awoke me from that dream.

Only thy youth, fair child, thy beauty, joy, and youth,
10 Can give me all I want, heart-ease and rest.

Though thou art ignorant of what dark books may hold,
  Or darker pages of real human life

Yet thou art not too young, too holy-innocent,
  To pity one in pain for human sin.

15 O Girl, a sole tear, shining on thy cheek for me
  More strengthens me than glittering angel-ranks;

Whose glory no eye sees; whose power is never felt,
  Whose sinlessness supports no sinful head,

Whose wondrous music never eased a human ear.
20 – Surely, because they are not, after all.

Ah, well-a-day; seeing my Heaven's empty now,
  I would the world were void of all but thee.

Oh, now, unless my face hath set too granite-hard
  And hurt thy tender hands to stroke it o'er,

25 Unless the fires that ever rage behind my eyes,
  Hot-sear thy lips in pressing kisses there,

    I crave thee, place thy two soft hands upon my cheeks,
        So shall long-treasured tears be loosed at last.

    Open thy infinite-vast eyes on me –
30   So shall my life melt out into their depth.

    And I shall die away content, without regret;
        Content to lose my sense of all for aye,

    Simply to live within the memory of thy mind;
        And when thy memory fail, to surcease, too.

35 Who would not part with life if he could surely know
        It might lie casketed in such a head?

Written at Dunsden in January 1913.

    21 well-a-day: Cp. Keats, 'The Eve of St. Agnes', l. 111: 'And as she muttered "Well-a – well-a-day!".'
    36 casketed: Cp. Keats, 'Isabella', ll. 431–2: 'So that the jewel, safely casketed, / Came forth, and in perfumèd leafits spread.'

MSS, p. 209

SONNET 3

Daily I muse on her; I muse and fret;
And take her little face between each hand;
But spare her – even imagined – kisses yet.
It is because, when first that face I scanned,
5   It wakened doubts I may no more forget,
And curious dreads I cannot understand.
They reach beyond the fears fond lovers pet,
That faith may change ere death; for they demand:

'What of her after Death? Shall we persist?
10 Will Death be merciful and keep her whole?'
In wonderment at this, I have not kissed;
And even now methought a whisper stole:
'Hast thou so learned Love's Law, and yet not wist
Her Beauty lives not? How, then, can her Soul?'

Written at Dunsden on 9 January 1913. One draft is dated 'Jan 9. 1912', but since it is on the same paper and in the same ink as a draft of No. 110, 'On My Songs' (p. 113), dated 'Jan 4 191$\frac{3}{2}$', it seems reasonable to assume that the other date should have been similarly emended. The subject of the poem is almost certainly a young Dunsden girl.

    4 Cp. Shakespeare, Sonnet 104, l. 2: 'when first your eye I ey'd'.
   11 Cp. No. 101, 'The Sleeping Beauty' (p. 104), ll. 11–14:
       So back I drew tiptoe from that Princess,
       Because it was too soon, and not my part,
       To start voluptuous pulses in her heart,
       And kiss her to the world of Consciousness.

MSS, p. 210

40   But it is not enough to look upon a rolling main,
      Forget, or half-forget, and look again,
      And so for ever.

      And it is not enough for me to view a fair campaign,
5   Forget, or half-forget, and view again,
      And so for ever.

      And it is not enough to gaze upon a nebule-streak,
      Forget, or half-forget, and gaze again,
      And so for ever.

10   And it is not enough to pore upon a woman's cheek,
      Forget, or half-forget, and pore again,
      And so for ever.

      But more I do not; neither hope to do. My life is vain.
      And I must languish till these memories wane,
15   And sleep for ever.

Written at Torquay on 20 April 1913, when WO was staying with his aunt, Edith Taylor (his uncle John having died in August 1912), these stanzas (from an unpublished letter to ELG) are prefaced: 'I have not visited T[eignmouth]. yet. Over Babbacombe cliffs I spent ten minutes extemporizing.' Following the poem, the letter continues: 'If there be anything in the above not deserving to sleep for ever, they are <u>safe with you</u>. I have already got too great a hoard of such wisps; and ~~nothing~~ not enough solid, presentable, cartload-poems.'

    7–9 nebule-streak . . . And so for ever: Cp. WO to SO, 26 April 1913: 'The same afternoon-rain fell the day before at Babbacombe. . . . We had to shelter for about two hours; but the Telescope I luckily gave to Colin acted as a talisman, potent as the Arabian Magician's Ivory Rod. For by feigning to see strange things through it (as indeed I did if mist and the blackness-of-darkness-for-ever are strange) I gathered five gentle children about me. . . .' (CL, 187) Cp. also No. 54, 'O World of many worlds, O life of lives' (p. 71).
    13 My life is vain: WO had left Dunsden in some distress in February 1913.

MS, p. 210

URICONIUM
An Ode

It lieth low near merry England's heart
Like a long-buried sin; and Englishmen
Forget that in its death their sires had part.
And, like a sin, Time lays it bare again
        To tell of races wronged,
And ancient glories suddenly overcast,
And treasures flung to fire and rabble wrath.
        If thou hast ever longed
To lift the gloomy curtain of Time Past,
And spy the secret things that Hades hath,
Here through this riven ground take such a view.
The dust, that fell unnoted as a dew,
Wrapped the dead city's face like mummy-cloth:
All is as was: except for worm and moth.

Since Jove was worshipped under Wrekin's shade
Or Latin phrase was writ in Shropshire stone,
Since Druid chaunts desponded in this glade
Or Tuscan general called that field his own,
        How long ago? How long?
How long since wanderers in the Stretton Hills
Met men of shaggy hair and savage jaw,
        With flint and copper prong,
Aiming behind their dikes and thorny grilles?
        Ah! those were days before the axe and saw,
        Then were the nights when this mid-forest town
        Held breath to hear the wolves come yelping down,
        And ponderous bears 'long Severn lifted paw,
        And nuzzling boars ran grunting through the shaw.

Ah me! full fifteen hundred times the wheat
Hath risen, and bowed, and fallen to human hunger
Since those imperial days were made complete.
The weary moon hath waxen old and younger
        These eighteen thousand times
Without a shrine to greet her gentle ray.
And other temples rose; to Power and Pelf,

And chimed centurial chimes
Until their very bells are worn away.
While King by King lay cold on vaulted shelf
And wars closed wars, and many a Marmion fell,
40 And dearths and plagues holp sire and son to hell;
And old age stiffened many a lively elf
And many a poet's heart outdrained itself.

I had forgot that so remote an age
Beyond the horizon of our little sight,
45 Is far from us by no more spanless gauge
Than day and night, succeeding day and night,
Until I looked on Thee,
Thou ghost of a dead city, or its husk!
But even as we could walk by field and hedge
50 Hence to the distant sea
So, by the rote of common dawn and dusk,
We travel back to history's utmost edge.
Yea, when through thy old streets I took my way,
And recked a thousand years as yesterday,
55 Methought sage fancy wrought a sacrilege
To steal for me such godly privilege!

For here lie remnants from a banquet table –
Oysters and marrow-bones, and seeds of grape –
The statement of whose age must sound a fable;
60 And Samian jars, whose sheen and flawless shape
Look fresh from potter's mould.
Plasters with Roman finger-marks impressed;
Bracelets, that from the warm Italian arm
Might seem to be scarce cold;
65 And spears – the same that pushed the Cymry west –
Unblunted yet; with tools of forge and farm
Abandoned, as a man in sudden fear
Drops what he holds to help his swift career:
For sudden was Rome's flight, and wild the alarm.
70 The Saxon shock was like Vesuvius' qualm.

O ye who prate of modern art and craft
Mark well that Gaulish brooch, and test that screw!

Art's fairest buds on antique stem are graft.
Under the sun is nothing wholly new!
      At Viricon today
The village anvil rests on Roman base
And in a garden, may be seen a bower
      With pillars for its stay
That anciently in basilic had place.
The church's font is but a pagan dower:
A Temple's column, hollowed into this.
So is the glory of our artifice,
Our pleasure and our worship, but the flower
Of Roman custom and of Roman power.

O ye who laugh and, living as if Time
Meant but the twelve hours ticking round your dial,
Find it too short for thee, watch the sublime,
Slow, epochal time-registers awhile,
      Which are Antiquities.
O ye who weep and call all your life too long
And moan: Was ever sorrow like to mine?
      Muse on the memories
That sad sepulchral stones and ruins prolong.
Here might men drink of wonder like strong wine
And feel ephemeral troubles soothed and curbed.
Yet farmers, wroth to have their laws disturbed,
Are sooner roused for little loss to pine
Than we are moved by mighty woes long syne.

Above this reverend ground, what traveller checks?
Yet cities such as these one time would breed
Apocalyptic visions of world-wrecks.
Let Saxon men return to them, and heed!
      They slew and burnt,
But after, prized what Rome had given away
Out of her strength and her prosperity.
      Have they yet learnt
The precious truth distilled from Rome's decay?
Ruins! On England's heart press heavily!
For Rome hath left us more than walls and words

110　And better yet shall leave; and more than herds
　　　Or land or gold gave the Celts to us in fee;
　　　E'en Blood, which makes poets sing and prophets see.

Written, probably at Shrewsbury, in July 1913 (wo, 88–90). Since August 1909, and perhaps earlier, WO had been a fascinated explorer of the remains of Uriconium, the Roman city at Wroxeter, on the Severn, east of Shrewsbury. The city and its inhabitants were destroyed by fire and sword *c.* A.D. 400. The first excavations were carried out in 1859–61, and the more important finds placed in the Shrewsbury Museum. WO and HO themselves collected several boxes full of shards. 'Uriconium / An Ode' owes a good deal to WO's copy of George Fox's *Guide to the Roman City of Uriconium* (1911).

　15　Wrekin's shade: The Wrekin is a hill ten miles to the east of Shrewsbury.
　28　shaw: thicket or small wood.
　39　Marmion: Lord Marmion, the hero of Scott's poem, *Marmion / A Tale of Flodden Field* (1808), was killed at the battle of Flodden in 1513.
　63　Cp. Keats, 'The Eve of St. Agnes', l. 228: 'Unclasps her warmèd jewels one by one'.
　65　the Cymry: the Welsh.
　70　Vesuvius' qualm: WO owned a copy of Bulwer-Lytton's *The Last Days of Pompeii* (1834), and in January 1909 wrote a lurid school essay on the subject of earthquakes and volcanic eruptions.
　91　Cp. Herbert, 'The Sacrifice', l. 4: 'Was ever grief like mine?'

MSS, p. 211

When late I viewed the gardens of rich men,
Where throve my darling blossoms plenteously,
With others whose rare glories dazed my ken,
I was not teased with envious misery.
Enough for me to see and recognize;
Then bear away sweet names upon my tongue,
Scents in my breath, and colours in my eyes.
Their owners watch them die: I keep them young.

But when more spacious pleasances I trod,
And saw their thousand buds, but might not kiss
Though loving like a lover, sire, and God,
Sad was the yearning of my avarice.
The rich man gives his parting guest one bloom,
But God hath vouchsafed my meek longing – whom?

Written in July–August 1913. Despite the disclaimer in WO's letter of mid-August 1913 to ELG that his sonnet 'was writ before Meols' (CL, 193), it clearly owes something to the handsome house and garden of his uncle Edward Quayle.

> 11 Cp. WO to SO, 29 January 1913: 'I can experience the happiness of paternity, fraternity, and amativeness all in one, sometimes' (CL, 180).

MSS, p. 211

53 Long ages past in Egypt thou wert worshipped
And thou wert wrought from ivory and beryl.
They brought thee jewels and they brought their slain,
Thy feet were dark with blood of sacrifice.
5 From dawn to midnight, O my painted idol,
Thou satest smiling, and the noise of killing
Was harp and timbrel in thy pale jade ears;
The livid dead were given thee for toys.

Thou wert a mad slave in a Persian palace,
10 And the King loved thee for thy furious beauty,
And all men heard thy ravings with a smile
Because thy face was fairer than a flower.
But with a little knife so wantonly
Thou slewest women and thy pining lovers,
15 And on thy lips the stain of crimson blood,
And on thy brow the pallor of their death.

Thou art the dream beheld by frenzied princes
In smoke of opium. Thou art the last fulfilment
Of all the wicked, and of all the beautiful.
20 We hold thee as a poppy to our mouths,
Finding with thee forgetfulness of God.
Thou art the face reflected in a mirror
Of wild desire, of pain, of bitter pleasure.
The witches shout thy name beneath the moon,
25 The fires of Hell have held thee in their fangs.

Fair-copied, according to the MS, on 31 October 1914 (WO, 111), this poem, notes Welland (42–3), 'is an invocation to an unspecified deity whose associations with passion, blood, and violent death prompt in the poet a frenzied exultation at this fusion of beauty and sin. Such, at least, seems to have been the intention, but the real motivation behind the poem seems to have been only a surfeit of Swinburne and Wilde, as is apparent from the heavily-accented alliteration, the reliance on a naïvely-employed sensuous imagery that recalls Wilde's "The Sphinx", and such phrases as "furious beauty", "wild desire", and "bitter pleasure".'

MSS, p. 212

O World of many worlds, O life of lives,
    What centre hast thou? Where am I?
O whither is it thy fierce onrush drives?
    Fight I, or drift; or stand; or fly?

5   The loud machinery spins, points work in touch;
    Wheels whirl in systems, zone in zone.
Myself, having sometime moved with such,
    Would strike a centre of mine own.

Lend hand, O Fate, for I am down, am lost!
10   Fainting by violence of the Dance . . .
Ah thanks, I stand – the floor is crossed,
    And I am where but few advance.

I see men far below me where they swarm . . .
    (Haply *above* me – be it so!
15 Does space to compass-points conform,
    And can we say a star stands high or low?)

Not more complex the millions of the stars
    Than are the hearts of mortal brothers;
As far remote as Neptune from small Mars
20   Is one man's nature from another's.

But all hold course unalterably fixed;
    They follow destinies foreplanned:
I envy not these lives their faith unmixed,
    I would not step with such a band.

25 To be a meteor, fast, eccentric, lone,
    Lawless; in passage through all spheres,
Warning the earth of wider ways unknown
    And rousing men with heavenly fears . . .

This is the track reserved for my endeavour;
30   Spanless the erring way I wend.
Blackness of darkness is my meed for ever?
    And barren plunging without end?

O glorious fear! Those other wandering souls
   High burning through that outer bourne
35 Are lights unto themselves. Fair aureoles
   Self-radiated there are worn.

And when in after times those stars return
   And strike once more earth's horizon,
They gather many satellites astern,
40 For they are greater than this system's Sun.

Begun at Dunsden, probably late in 1912, and continued in France between October and December 1914. 'Perhaps the Vicar [of Dunsden] drew Owen's attention to St. Jude's ferocious condemnation of heretical and worldly men within the Church who were "Raging waves of the sea, foaming out their own shame; wandering stars, to whom is reserved the blackness of darkness for ever"' (DH, 31). WO quoted this passage from Jude 13 in his letter of 26 April 1913 to SO: 'the Telescope I luckily gave to Colin acted as a talisman, potent as the Arabian Magician's Ivory Rod. For by feigning to see strange things through it (as indeed I did if mist and the blackness-of-darkness-for-ever are strange) I gathered five gentle children about me. . . .' (CL, 187)

    1 Cp. Shelley, 'O World, O Life, O Time'; and Tagore, *Gitanjali*, poem 12, ll. 3–6:
> I came out on the chariot of the first
> gleam of light, and pursued my voyage
> through the wilderness of worlds, leaving
> my track on many a star and planet.

   11 the floor: Cp. Keats, 'The Fall of Hyperion', l. 234: 'the pavèd floor'.

   25 meteor: Cp. WO to SS, 5 November 1917: 'And you have <u>fixed</u> my Life – however short. You did not light me: I was always a mad comet; but you have fixed me. I spun round you a satellite for a month, but I shall swing out soon, a dark star in the orbit where you will blaze. It is some consolation to know that Jupiter himself sometimes swims out of Ken!' (CL, 505)

33–6 Cp. Shelley, 'Adonais', ll. 492–5:
> I am born darkly, fearfully, afar;
> Whilst burning through the inmost veil of Heaven,
> The soul of Adonais, like a star,
> Beacons from the abode where the Eternal are.

MSS, p. 213

The time was aeon; and the place all earth.
The spectacle I saw was not a dream,
But true resumption of experienced things.
The scene meseemed one vast deformity,
5 Made lovely by pervasion of a spirit.
For as the morning sunshine sanctifies
Even the ordure of a sordid town,
So all this wreck was glamoured by some charm
A mystery of music. For, a Presence there
10 Created low, rich music, endlessly.
The Place was called the World, and lo! the name
Of him, the unapparent spirit, was
An evil Angel's; and I learnt the name
Of that strange, regnant Presence as the Flesh.
15 It bore the naked likeness of a boy
Flawlessly moulded, fine exceedingly,
Beautiful unsurpassably – so much
More portraiture were fond futility
For even thought is not long possible,
20 Becoming too soon passion: and meseemed
His outline changed, from beauty unto beauty,
As change the contours of slim, sleeping clouds.
His skin, too, glowed, pale scarlet like the clouds
Lit from the eastern underworld; which thing
25 Bewondered me the more. But I remember
The statue of his body standing so
Against the huge disorder of the place
Resembled a strong music; and it triumphed
Even as the trend of one clear perfect air
30 Across confusion of a thousand chords.
Then watched I how there ran towards that way
A multitude of railers, hot with hate,
And maddened by the voice of a small Jew
Who cried with a loud voice, saying 'Away!
35 Away with him!' and 'Crucify him! Him,
With the affections and the lusts thereof.'

Begun, probably at Dunsden, in 1912/13 (WO, 70–1); a heavily corrected fair copy headed 'Final Version' was made at Mérignac in summer 1915. 'The small Jew is St. Paul, urging his followers to "crucify the flesh" (Galatians 5: 24). It is clear from the passionate tone of the description that the poet's sympathies lie entirely with "the Flesh" and not at all with St Paul.' (DH, *Wilfred Owen* [Writers and Their Work, 1975], 10) 'Read out of context, this clumsy and over-written piece might be taken as some kind of homosexual fantasy. It becomes less odd, however, when it is recognized as an imitation of [Harold] Monro's prophetic style and a reworking of the symbolic "Titan of the dawn – Humanity" which is described in the opening poem of *Before Dawn*:

> His visionary eyes looked out afar
>   Beyond the transient semblances of death.
> No sound of supplication came to mar
>
> The rhythm of his calmly-taken breath.
>   No ripple of a thin or faint delight
> Moved round his crimson lips; and underneath
>
> His bright skin aureoled by the rose twilight
>   Rolled the vast torrent of majestic thews.
> Master of his strong passion . . .'

(DH, 'Wilfred Owen and the Georgians', RES, n.s., xxx, no. 117 [1979], 28–40)

    21 Cp. Wesley, 'Love Divine, all loves excelling', ll. 21–2: 'changed from glory into glory, / Till in heaven we take our place. . . .'

MS, p. 216

NOCTURNE

Now, as the warm approach of honied slumber blurs my sense,
Before I yield me to th'enchantment of my bed,
God rest all souls in toil and turbulence,
All men a-weary seeking bread;
5   God rest them all tonight!
Let sleep expunge
The day's monotonous vistas from their sight;
And let them plunge
Deep down the dusky firmament of reverie
10   And drowse of dreams with me.

Ah! I should drowse away the night most peacefully
But that there toil too many bodies unreposed
Who fain would fall on lethargy;
Too many leaden eyes unclosed;
15   And aching hands amove
Interminably,
Beneath the light that night will not remove;
Too many brains that rave in dust and steam!
They rave, but cannot dream!

Written at Mérignac between June and August 1915.

MS, p. 217

64 IMPROMPTU

Now, let me feel the feeling of thy hand –
For it is softer than the breasts of girls,
And warmer than the pillows of their cheeks,
And richer than the fullness of their eyes,
5 And stronger than the ardour of their hearts.

Its shape is subtler than a dancer's limbs;
Its skin is coloured like the twilight Alp;
And odoured like the pale, night-scented flowers,
And fresh with early love, as earth with dawn.

10 Yield me thy hand a little while, fair love;
That I may feel it; and so feel thy life,
And kiss across it, as the sea the sand,
And love it, with the love of Sun for Earth.

Ah! let me look a long while in thine eyes,
15 For they are deeper than the depths of thought,
And clearer than the ether after rain,
And suaver than the moving of the moon,
And vaster than the void of all desire.

Child, let me fully see and know those eyes!
20 Their fire is like the wrath of shaken rubies;
Their shade is like the peaceful forest-heart.

They hold me as the great star holds the less.
I see them as the lights beyond this life.
They reach me by a sense not found in man,
25 And bless me with a bliss unguessed of God.

Written in Bordeaux between June and August 1915; ll. 1–13 were incorporated in a letter to ELG (CL, 343–4).

6–9 Cp. No. 117, 'From My Diary, July 1914' (p. 120).

MSS, p. 218

A PALINODE

Some little while ago, I had a mood
When what we know as 'Nature' seemed to me
So sympathetic, ample, sweet, and good
That I preferred it to Society.

5 Not for a season, be it understood,
But altogether and perpetually.
As far as feeling went, I thought I could
Be quit of men, live independently.

For men and minds, heart-humours and heart's-tease
10 Disturbed without exciting: whereas woods,
The seasonal changes, and the chanting seas
Were both soul-rousing and sense-lulling. Moods,

Such moods prolonged, became a mania.
I found the stark stretch of a bleak-blown moor
15 Least barren of all places. Mere extranea
Seemed populace and town: things to ignore.

But if the sovereign sun I might behold
With condescension coming down benign,
And blessing all the field and air with gold,
20 Then the contentment of the world was mine.

In secret deserts where the night was nude
And each excited star grew ardent-eyed,
I tasted more than this life's plenitude,
And far as farthest stars perceive, I spied.

25 Once, when the whiteness of the spectral moon
Had terrorized the creatures of the wold,
When that long staring of the glazed-eyed
Had stupefied the land and made it cold,

I fell seduced into a madness; for,
30 Forgetting in that night the life of days,
I said I had no need of fellows more,
I madly hated men and all their ways.

　　　　I hated, feeling hated; I supposed
　　　　That others did not need me any more.
35　　The book of human knowledge I then closed;
　　　　Passion, art, science? Trifles to ignore.

　　　　But in my error, men ignored not me,
　　　　And did not let me in my moonbeams bask.
　　　　And I took antidotes; though what they be
40　　Unless yourself be poisoned, do not ask.

　　　　For I am overdosed. The City now
　　　　Holds all my passion; these my soul most feels:
　　　　Crowds surging; racket of traffic; market row;
　　　　Bridges, sonorous under rapid wheels;

45　　Pacific lamentations of a bell;
　　　　The smoking of the old men at their doors;
　　　　All attitudes of children; the farewell
　　　　And casting-off of ships for far-off shores.

Written, or at any rate fair-copied, in London in October 1915. The wording of ll. 37–40 would appear to indicate a sexual awakening behind the change of heart that occasions the palinode ('Poem in which author retracts thing said in former poem, recantation', *SOED*).

　　11　Cp. John Drinkwater, 'The Fires of God', v, l. 164: 'And the great hills and solemn chanting seas'.

　　19　Cp. No. 177, 'Spring Offensive' (p. 192), l. 15. The evolution of the phrase 'blessed with gold' is discussed in wo, 44.

　　25　Cp. Meredith, *Modern Love*, xxxix: 'God, what a dancing spectre seems the moon.' WO had been given a copy of Meredith's *Poems* (1910) in May 1912 (CL, 136 and 141).

　　27　Cp. No. 82, 'Perseus' (p. 464), and No. 14, 'Supposed Confessions of a Secondrate Sensitive Mind in Dejection' (p. 13), ll. 20–1.

　44–5　These lines were incorporated with only slight changes in No. 92, 'I know the music' (p. 485). Cp. Flaubert, *Madame Bovary*, part II, chap. VI: 'et la cloche, sonnant toujours, continuait dans les airs sa lamentation pacifique'.

MS, p. 218

It was a navy boy, so prim, so trim,
That boarded my compartment of the train.
    I shared my cigarettes and books to him.
    He shared his heart to me. (Who knows my gain!)

(His head was golden like the oranges
That catch their brightness from Las Palmas sun.)
    'O whence and whither bound, lad?' 'Home,' he says,
    'Home, from Hong Kong, sir, and a ten months' run.'

(His blouse was all as blue as morning sea,
His face was fresh like dawn above that blue.)
    'I got one letter, sir, just one,' says he,
    'And no shore-leave out there, sir, for the crew.'

(His look was noble as a good ship's prow
And all of him was clean as pure east wind.)
    'I am no "sir", I said, 'but tell me now
    What carried you? Not tea, nor tamarind?'

Strong were his silken muscles hiddenly
As under currents where the waters smile.
    'Nitre we carried. By next week maybe
    That should be winning France another mile.'

His words were shapely, even as his lips,
And courtesy he used like any lord.
    'Was it through books that you first thought of ships?'
    'Reading a book, sir, made me go aboard.

'Another hour and I'll be home,' he said.
(His eyes were happy even as his heart.)
    'Twenty-five pounds I'm taking home,' he said,
    'It's five miles there; and I shall run, best part.'

And as we talked, some things he said to me
Not knowing, cleansed me of a cowardice,
    As I had braced me in the dangerous sea.
    Yet I should scarce have told it but for this.

'Those pounds,' I said. 'You'll put some twenty by?'
'All for my mother, sir.' And turned his head.
35   'Why all?' I asked, in pain that he should sigh:
'Because I must. She needs it most,' he said.

Written in London in late October or early November 1915.

19   nitre: sodium nitrate, a chemical component of certain explosives.

MSS, p. 219

68

Whereas most women live this difficult life
Merely in order not to die the death
And take experience as they take their breath,
Accepting backyards, travail, crusts, all naïf;
And nothing greatly love, and nothing loathe –
Others there are who seemingly forget
That men build walls to shelter from the wet,
For sustenance take meals, for comfort clothe.

These must embellish every act with grace;
These eat for savours; dress to show their lace;
Suppose the earth for gardens; hands for nard.
Now which you hold as higher than the other
Depends, in fine, on whether you regard
The poetess as nobler than the Mother.

Probably written in 1915, this sonnet exists only in a transcript from a MS since lost.

Transcript, p. 222

72 A NEW HEAVEN
(To —— on Active Service)

    Seeing we never found gay fairyland
      (Though still we crouched by bluebells moon by moon)
    And missed the tide of Lethe; yet are soon
      For that new bridge that leaves old Styx half-spanned;
5   Nor ever unto Mecca caravanned;
      Nor bugled Asgard, skilled in magic rune;
    Nor yearned for far Nirvana, the sweet swoon,
      And from high Paradise are cursed and banned;

    – Let's die home, ferry across the Channel! Thus
10 Shall we live gods there. Death shall be no sev'rance.
    Weary cathedrals light new shrines for us.
      To us, rough knees of boys shall ache with rev'rence.
    Are not girls' breasts a clear, strong Acropole?
    – There our own mothers' tears shall heal us whole.

Composed probably at Witley and, according to one dated MS, in September 1916.

TITLE Taken from Revelation 31:1, 'And I saw a new heaven and a new earth: for the first heaven and the first earth were passed away.'

DEDICATION The unnamed soldier has not been identified.

    3 Lethe: In Greek mythology, a river through Hades the taste of whose waters caused forgetfulness of the past.

    4 Styx: In Greek mythology, the boundary river encircling Hades.

    6 Asgard: In Norse mythology, the abode of the gods, accessible only by the bridge Bifrost.

    9 The MS reads: ' – Let's die home, ferry home across the Channel! Thus'. I have omitted the second 'home' on the grounds that it is both tautological and involves an uncharacteristic expansion of the pentameter line.

11–14 An anticipation of No. 96, 'Anthem for Doomed Youth' (p. 99), ll. 9–12:

    What candles may be held to speed them all?
      Not in the hands of boys but in their eyes
    Shall shine the holy glimmers of goodbyes.
      The pallor of girls' brows shall be their pall.

    13 Acropole: WO introduces the French word for 'Acropolis', the highest, and usually fortified, part of a Greek city. He was presumably thinking of the Acropolis at Athens, which is built of white marble, but not domed as his image would seem to suggest.

MSS, p. 222

74 STORM

His face was charged with beauty as a cloud
   With glimmering lightning. When it shadowed me,
   I shook, and was uneasy as a tree
That draws the brilliant danger, tremulous, bowed.

5 So must I tempt that face to loose its lightning.
   Great gods, whose beauty is death, will laugh above,
   Who made his beauty lovelier than love.
I shall be bright with their unearthly brightening.

And happier were it if my sap consume;
10 Glorious will shine the opening of my heart;
The land shall freshen that was under gloom;
What matter if all men cry out and start,
And women hide their faces in their shawl,
At those hilarious thunders of my fall?

Written, according to the dated MS, in October 1916 (WO, 139).

    12 Cp. Shelley, 'Ode to Liberty', ll. 164–5: 'Men started, staggering with a glad surprise, / Under the lightnings of thine unfamiliar eyes.'
    14 hilarious: 'WO's poems are full of strange references to laughter. Cp. l. 6 above and [No. 148] "Strange Meeting", l. 22' (DH, 112).

MS, p. 225

75 TO THE BITTER SWEET-HEART: A DREAM

    One evening Eros took me by the hand,
    And having folded feathers round my head,
    Or sleep like feathers, towards a far hope sped,
    I groping, for he bade me understand
5   He would soon fill with Yours my other hand –
    But when I heard his singing wings expand
    My face fell deeply in his shoulder.
    Sweet moons we flew thus, yet I waned not older
    But in his exquisiteness I flagged, unmanned
10 Till, when his wings were drooping to an end
    Feeling my empty hand fulfilled with His,
    I knew Love gave himself my passion-friend.
    So my old quest of you requited is,
    Ampler than e'er I asked of your girl's grace.
15 I shall not ask you more, nor see your face.

Written in France early in 1917.

  1 Eros: Cp. No. 112, 'To Eros' (p. 115).

MS, p. 225

ROUNDEL

In Shrewsbury Town e'en Hercules wox tired,
Tired of the streets that end not up nor down;
Tired of the Quarry, though seats may be hired
           Of Shrewsbury Town.

5 Tired of the tongues that knew not his renown;
Tired of the Quarry Bye-Laws, so admired
By the Salopian, the somnambulant clown.

Weak as a babe, and in like wise attired,
He leaned upon his club; frowned a last frown,
10 And of ineffable boredom, so expired
           In Shrewsbury Town.

Written probably at the Casualty Clearing Station in May 1917 (rather than at Bordeaux in May 1914, as the editors of CL suggest), this rondel appears in a letter to ELG where it is prefaced: 'I thought I would try a Roundel. I find it exceedingly easy to write one without having either emotion or ideas. Thus: Roundel on the Statue of Hercules reposing from his Labours in the Quarry, Shrewsbury.' (CL, 250).

    1 Hercules: Cp. WO's treatment of the combat between Hercules and Antaeus, No. 138, 'The Wrestlers' (p. 520).

MS, p. 225

79 HOW DO I LOVE THEE?

I cannot woo thee as the lion his mate,
With proud parade and fierce prestige of presence;
Nor thy fleet fancy may I captivate
With pastoral attitudes in flowery pleasance;
5 Nor will I kneeling court thee with sedate
And comfortable plans of husbandhood;
Nor file before thee as a candidate. . . .
I cannot woo thee as a lover would.

To wrest thy hand from rivals, iron-gloved,
10 Or cheat them by a craft, I am not clever.
But I do love thee even as Shakespeare loved,
Most gently wild, and desperately for ever,
Full-hearted, grave, and manfully in vain,
With thought, high pain, and ever vaster pain.

Written probably at the Casualty Clearing Station in May 1917, this poem is mentioned in the postscript to WO's letter to ELG tentatively dated '? late May 1914' by the editors of CL (250–1). The opening page/s of this is/are missing and internal evidence suggests 1917 as a more likely date.

TITLE Cp. Elizabeth Barrett Browning, *Sonnets from the Portuguese*, 43: 'How do I love thee? Let me count the ways.'

Transcript, p. 226

THE FATES

They watch me, those informers to the Fates
Called Fortune, Chance, Necessity, and Death;
Time, in disguise as one who serves and waits,
Eternity as girls of fragrant breath.
5 I know them. Men and Boys are in their pay,
And those I hold my trustiest friends may prove
Agents of Theirs to take me if I stray
From fatal ordinance. If I move, they move –

Escape? There is one unwatched way; your eyes,
10 O Beauty! Keep me good that secret gate!
And when the cordon tightens of the spies
Let the close iris of your eyes grow great.
So I'll evade the vice and rack of age
And miss the march of lifetime, stage by stage.

Written at Craiglockhart on 31 June / 1 July 1917. On 1 July WO wrote to ELG: 'Late last night I very hastily draughted a Fate sonnet. I had an Idea – which is almost my Gospel. Can you get it from this? If so, how would you express it in prose?' (CL, 473). A '2nd Draught' of 'The Fates' followed.

    3 one who serves and waits: Cp. Milton, 'When I Consider How My Light Is Spent', l. 14: 'They also serve who only stand and wait.'
13–14 Cp. No. 148, 'Strange Meeting' (p. 148), l. 32: 'To miss the march of this retreating world'.

MSS, p. 226

85 HAPPINESS

Ever again to breathe pure happiness,
So happy that we gave away our toy?
We smiled at nothings, needing no caress?
Have we not laughed too often since with Joy?
5 Have we not stolen too strange and sorrowful wrongs
For her hands' pardoning? The sun may cleanse,
And time, and starlight. Life will sing great songs,
And gods will show us pleasures more than men's.

Yet heaven looks smaller than the old doll's-home,
10 No nestling place is left in bluebell bloom,
And the wide arms of trees have lost their scope.
The former happiness is unreturning:
Boys' griefs are not so grievous as youth's yearning,
Boys have no sadness sadder than our hope.

Begun at Abbeville in February 1917, this poem was one of several written on a 'subject' agreed by WO, ELG, and their mutual friend Olwen Joergens (wo, 161–3). For a fuller account of these competitive compositions, see DH, '"Rival Pieces on a Chosen Theme": A Note on Some of Wilfred Owen's Minor Poems', *Four Decades of Poetry 1890–1930* (Merseyside), i, no. 1 (January 1976), 70–5. WO writes of Miss Joergens's poem 'Happiness' in his letter to SO of 12 February 1917 (CL, 434), and on 25 February he tells his mother: 'My "Happiness" is dedicated to you. It contains perhaps two good lines. Between you an' me the sentiment is all bilge. Or nearly all. But I think it makes a creditable Sonnet. You must not conclude I have misbehaved in any way from the tone of the poem (though you might infer it if you knew the tone of this Town.) On the contrary I have been a very good boy. . . .' (CL, 437). Sometime between late June and August he revised the poem at Craiglockhart, writing to SO on 8 August 1917: '(Not before January 1917 did I write the only lines of mine that carry the stamp of maturity: these:
   But the old happiness is unreturning.
   Boys have no grief so grievous as youth's yearning;
   Boys have no sadness sadder than our hope.)' (CL, 482)

MSS, p. 227

86 SONG OF SONGS

Sing me at dawn but only with your laugh:
    Like sprightly Spring that laugheth into leaf;
    Like Love, that cannot flute for smiling at Life.

Sing to me only with your speech all day,
    As voluble leaflets do. Let viols die.
    The least word of your lips is melody.

Sing me at dusk, but only with your sigh;
    Like lifting seas it solaceth: breathe so,
    All voicelessly, the sense that no songs say.

Sing me at midnight with your murmurous heart;
    And let its moaning like a chord be heard
    Surging through you and sobbing unsubdued.

Written sometime between late June and mid-August 1917 (WO, 210–11). On 23 August 1917 WO told ELG of his first meeting with SS: 'Some of my old Sonnets didn't please him at all. But the "Antaeus" he applauded fervently; and a short lyric which I don't think you know "Sing me at morn but only with thy Laugh" he pronounced perfect work, absolutely charming, etc. etc. and begged that I would copy it out for him, to show to the powers that be.' (CL, 486) The poem was printed in *The Hydra*, 1 September 1917, and in May 1918 it received a consolation prize in a lyric competition organized by *The Bookman*. By then, however, WO had outgrown it, writing to SO on 29 May 1918: 'The *Bookman* affair about which you are so kindly importunate was a mere idle joke, an old lyric I condescended to send from Scarboro'' (CL, 554). The poem has marked affinities with No. 117, 'From My Diary, July 1914' (p. 120).

    1 Cp. Jonson, 'Song: To Celia', l. 1: 'Drink to me only with thine eyes'.

MS, p. 230

88   Has your soul sipped
        Of the sweetness of all sweets?
   Has it well supped
        But yet hungers and sweats?

5   I have been witness
        Of a strange sweetness,
   All fancy surpassing
        Past all supposing.

   Passing the rays
10   Of the rubies of morning,
   Or the soft rise
        Of the moon; or the meaning
   Known to the rose
        Of her mystery and mourning.

15   Sweeter than nocturnes
        Of the wild nightingale
   Or than love's nectar
        After life's gall.

   Sweeter than odours
20   Of living leaves,
   Sweeter than ardours
        Of dying loves.

   Sweeter than death
        And dreams hereafter
25   To one in dearth
        Of life and its laughter.

   Or the proud wound
        The victor wears
   Or the last end
30   Of all wars.

   Or the sweet murder
        After long guard
   Unto the martyr
        Smiling at God;

35 To me was that smile,
    Faint as a wan, worn myth,
Faint and exceeding small,
    On a boy's murdered mouth.

Though from his throat
40   The life-tide leaps
There was no threat
    On his lips.

But with the bitter blood
    And the death-smell
45 All his life's sweetness bled
    Into a smile.

Written at Craiglockhart in July-August 1917, this would seem to be one of WO's first experiments in sustained pararhyme. Five of the rhyme words and 'nocturnes' (l. 15) appear in a long list of pararhymes pencilled on the back of a draft of No. 47, 'The Imbecile' (p. 429), written in Bordeaux in 1913. On the back of the last MS page of 'Has your soul sipped' WO has written: 'Marlboro' & Other Poems / <u>Chas Sorely</u>'. Sorley's book was published in January 1916.

MSS, p. 232

89 THE SWIFT
An Ode

   When the blue has broken
    Through the pearly heat
   And the grass is woken
    By our early feet,
Oh, then to be the Lark! – With all his fun
To pelt my mate with gayest kisses,
And mount to laugh away those blisses
In shaking merriment unto the sun!

   When the dark is listening
    And the leaves hang still,
   While the glow-worms, glistening,
    Make the keen stars thrill,
Would I might mourn to one lorn Nightingale
And be the solace of her solitude,
Speaking my doles all clear and unsubdued
And audible to her, the Nightingale.

   But when eve shines lowly,
    And the light is thinned,
   And the moon slides slowly
    Down the far-off wind,
Oh, then to be of all the birds the Swift!
To flit through ether, with elves winging,
Drawn up western fires, in frenzy singing,
Along the breeze to lean and poise and drift!

   Fine thou art and agile,
    O thou perfect bird,
   As an arrow fragile
    By an Eros whirred;
And like a cross-bow in a Cupid's grasp
Thy wings are ever stretched, for striking ready;
And like young Love thou'rt frantic and unsteady,
And sure as his thine aim, and keen as Love's thy gasp.

        Strung in tautest tension
            By the lust of speed,
        And the mad contention
            Of insatiate greed,
Thou suck'st away the intoxicating air,
Trailing a wake of song in trilling bubbles,
Till distance drowns thee. Then thy light wing doubles,
And thou art back, – nay vanished now, Oh where?

        Down in sharp declension,
            Grazing the low pool;
        Up in steep ascension
            Where the clouds blow cool;
And there thou sleepest all the luminous night,
Aloft this hurry and this hunger,
Floating with years that knew thee younger,
Without this nest to feed, this death to fight.

        Airily sweeping and swinging,
            Quivering unstable,
        Like a dark butterfly clinging
            To the roof-gable,
Art thou not tired of this unceasing round?
Long'st not for rest in mead or bower?
Must lose, as spirits lose, the power
To soar again if once thou come to ground?

        Waywardly sliding and slinging,
            Speed never slacking,
        Easily, recklessly flinging,
            Twinkling and tacking;
– Oh, how we envy thee thy lovely swerves!
How covet we thy slim wings' beauty,
Nor guess what stress of need and duty
So bent thy frame to those slim faultless curves.

        Dazzlingly swooping and plunging
            Into the nest to peep,
        Dangerously leaping and lunging –
            Hark! how the younglings cheep!

O Swift! If thou art master of the air
70 Who taught thee! Not the joy of flying
But of thy brood: their throttles' crying
Stung thee to skill whereof men yet despair!

    Desperately driving and dashing,
        Hissing and shrieking,
75   Breathlessly hurtling and lashing,
        Seeking and seeking,
What knowest thou of grace or dance or song?
Thy cry that ringeth like a lyric,
Is it indeed of joy, a panegyric?
80 No ecstasy is this. By love's pain it rings strong.

    O that I might make me
        Pinions like to thine,
    Feathers that would take me
        Whither I incline!
85 Yet more thy spirit's tirelessness I crave;
Yet more thy joyous fierce endurance.
If my soul flew with thy assurance,
What fields, what skies to scour! What seas to brave!

Drafted at Dunsden in the early summer of 1912, after WO had proposed to ELG one evening that they should each write a poem on the subject of 'The Swift' (WO, 73, and DH, '"Rival Pieces on a Chosen Theme": A Note on Some of Wilfred Owen's Minor Poems', *Four Decades of Poetry 1890–1930* [Merseyside], i, no. 1 [January 1976], 70). The poem was revised in Bordeaux between June and August 1915, and further revised at Craiglockhart in August 1917, probably before WO came under the influence of SS.

MSS, p. 234

INSPECTION

'You! What d'you mean by this?' I rapped.
'You dare come on parade like this?'
'Please, sir, it's – ' ' 'Old yer mouth,' the sergeant snapped.
'I takes 'is name, sir?' – 'Please, and then dismiss.'

5 Some days 'confined to camp' he got,
For being 'dirty on parade'.
He told me, afterwards, the damnèd spot
Was blood, his own. 'Well, blood is dirt,' I said.

'Blood's dirt,' he laughed, looking away,
10 Far off to where his wound had bled
And almost merged for ever into clay.
'The world is washing out its stains,' he said.
'It doesn't like our cheeks so red:
Young blood's its great objection.
15 But when we're duly white-washed, being dead,
The race will bear Field Marshal God's inspection.'

Drafted at Craiglockhart in August 1917 and completed in September, this shows the influence of SS (cp. 'They').

> 7 damnèd spot: A reference to *Macbeth*, v. i. 35: 'Out, damnèd spot!' This 'deliberately recalls the occasion of Lady Macbeth's sleepwalking when blood was indeed dirt – the irremovable dirt of guilt – and the association is sustained a few lines later by the reference to the washing out of stains, but the same image also carries a sacrificial overtone ("Are you washed in the Blood of the Lamb?") which anticipates the grim irony of the final lines' (Welland, 62).
>
> 15 The whitewashing of military installations, kerbstones, etc., was a form of superficial cleaning resented by British troops and the target of much sarcasm. 'Pipe clay', a form of white clay, is applied with water to whiten soldiers' webbing equipment.

MSS, p. 240

91 WITH AN IDENTITY DISC

If ever I had dreamed of my dead name
High in the heart of London, unsurpassed
By Time for ever, and the Fugitive, Fame,
There taking a long sanctuary at last,

5 I better that; and recollect with shame
How once I longed to hide it from life's heats
Under those holy cypresses, the same
That keep in shade the quiet place of Keats.

Now, rather, thank I God there is no risk
10 Of gravers scoring it with florid screed,
But let my death be memoried on this disc.
Wear it, sweet friend. Inscribe no date nor deed.
But let thy heart-beat kiss it night and day,
Until the name grow vague and wear away.

Drafted on 23 March 1917, a preliminary fair copy of this sonnet accompanied WO's letter to CO the following day (WO, **175**–6). In this he wrote: 'I will send you my last Sonnet, which I started yesterday. I think I will address it to you. *Adieu, mon petit. Je t'embrasse.*' (CL, 446) The poem was revised at Craiglockhart in August–September 1917. It shows the influence of Shakespeare's Sonnet 104, 'To me, fair friend, you never can be old', that in March 1917 WO had copied from memory into the notebook in which he drafted his own, and Keats's sonnet, 'When I have fears that I may cease to be'. Previous editors print an earlier version of ll. 4–8 and emendations proposed by SS to ll. 11 and 14.

> TITLE A British soldier was issued with three identity discs bearing his name and number. They were worn on a cord round his neck and, if he was killed, one was sent to his next of kin.
>
> 2 References to Westminster in the MSS indicate that WO had in mind a memorial in Poets' Corner, Westminster Abbey.
>
> 7–8 Keats is buried among cypress trees in the Protestant Cemetery at Rome.

MSS, p. 241

THE PROMISERS

When I awoke, the glancing day looked gay;
The air said: Fare you fleetly; you will meet him!
And when the prosp'rous sun was well begun,
I heard a bird say: Sweetly you shall greet him!

5 The sun fell strong and bold upon my shoulder;
It hung, it clung as it were my friend's arm.
The birds fifed on before, shrill-piping pipers,
Right down to town; and there they ceased to charm.

And there I wandered till the noon came soon,
10 And chimed: The time is hastening with his face!
Sly twilight said: I bring him; wait till late!
But darkness harked forlorn to my lone pace.

Written at Craiglockhart, probably between August and October 1917.

MSS, p. 245

95 MUSIC

    I have been urged by earnest violins
       And drunk their mellow sorrows to the slake
    Of all my sorrows and my thirsting sins.
       My heart has beaten for a brave drum's sake.
5   Huge chords have wrought me mighty: I have hurled
       Thuds of gods' thunder. And with old winds pondered
    Over the curse of this chaotic world, –
       With low lost winds that maundered as they wandered.

    I have been gay with trivial fifes that laugh;
10 And songs more sweet than possible things are sweet;
    And gongs, and oboes. Yet I guessed not half
    Life's symphony till I had made hearts beat,
    And touched Love's body into trembling cries,
    And blown my love's lips into laughs and sighs.

Begun in October 1916, according to a dated MS, this poem was one of several written on a 'subject' agreed by WO, ELG, and their mutual friend Olwen Joergens (WO, 161–2). For a fuller account of these competitive compositions, see DH, '"Rival Pieces on a Chosen Theme": A Note on Some of Wilfred Owen's Minor Poems', *Four Decades of Poetry 1890–1930* (Merseyside), i, no. 1 (January 1976), 70–5. The poem was revised at Craiglockhart, and evidently shown to SS, between August and November 1917. For a discussion of 'Music' and its links with No. 55, 'Nights with the Wind. A Rhapsody' (p. 439), see Bäckman, 129–31.

    6 gods':   EB and CDL read 'God's', for which there is no MS authority.

MSS, p. 246

ANTHEM FOR DOOMED YOUTH

What passing-bells for these who die as cattle?
 – Only the monstrous anger of the guns.
 Only the stuttering rifles' rapid rattle
Can patter out their hasty orisons.
No mockeries now for them; no prayers nor bells;
 Nor any voice of mourning save the choirs, –
The shrill, demented choirs of wailing shells;
 And bugles calling for them from sad shires.

What candles may be held to speed them all?
 Not in the hands of boys but in their eyes
Shall shine the holy glimmers of goodbyes.
 The pallor of girls' brows shall be their pall;
Their flowers the tenderness of patient minds,
And each slow dusk a drawing-down of blinds.

Written at Craiglockhart in September–October 1917 (WO, **217**–22). SS helped with the revision of the poem and, on 25 September, WO wrote to SO: 'I send you my two best war Poems. Sassoon supplied the title "Anthem": just what I meant it to be.' (CL, 496)

> 1 passing-bells: WO was probably responding to the anonymous Prefatory Note to *Poems of Today: an Anthology* (1916), of which he possessed the December 1916 reprint: 'This book has been compiled in order that boys and girls, already perhaps familiar with the great classics of the English speech, may also know something of the newer poetry of their own day. Most of the writers are living, and the rest are still vivid memories among us, while one of the youngest, almost as these words are written, has gone singing to lay down his life for his country's cause. . . . there is no arbitrary isolation of one theme from another; they mingle and interpenetrate throughout, to the music of Pan's flute, and of Love's viol, and the bugle-call of Endeavour, and the passing-bells of Death.'
>
> 2 Cp. No. 93, 'But I was looking at the permanent stars' (p. 488): 'The monstrous anger of our taciturn guns'.
>
> 6–7 Cp. Keats, 'To Autumn', l. 27: 'Then in a wailful choir the small gnats mourn.'
>
> 7 Cp. WO to SO, 2 April 1916: 'The fifers are worthy to rank with the demented violins that make Queen's Hall to spin round as a top, and with the Cathedral Choir that pierces thro' the heights of heaven' (CL, 388).

8 Cp. No. 92, 'I know the music' (p. 485): 'Bugles that sadden all the evening air'; and No. 93, 'But I was looking at the permanent stars' (p. 487): 'Bugles sang, saddening the evening air.'

10–11 Cp. Yeats, *Poems* (1895), 'The Wanderings of Oisin', II. 69: 'A maiden with soft eyes like funeral tapers'.

10–13 Cp. No. 72, 'A New Heaven' (p. 82), ll. 11–13:
Weary cathedrals light new shrines for us.
  To us, rough knees of boys shall ache with rev'rence.
Are not girls' breasts a clear, strong Acropole?

14 Cp. Laurence Binyon, 'For the Fallen', ll. 15–16: 'At the going down of the sun and in the morning / We will remember them.' DH notes: 'Drawing down the blinds of a house, now an almost forgotten custom, indicated either that a funeral procession was passing or that there had been a death in the house. It was customary to keep the coffin in the house until taking it to church; it would be placed in the darkened parlour, with a pall and flowers on it and lighted candles nearby. Relatives and friends would enter the room to pay their last respects. The sestet of the poem, in fact, refers to a household in mourning.' (DH, 147)

MSS, p. 249

WINTER SONG

The browns, the olives, and the yellows died,
And were swept up to heaven; where they glowed
Each dawn and set of sun till Christmastide.
And when the land lay pale for them, pale-snowed,
5 Fell back, and down the snow-drifts flamed and flowed.

From off your face, into the winds of winter,
The sun-brown and the summer-gold are blowing;
But they shall gleam again with spiritual glinter,
When paler beauty on your brows falls snowing,
10 And through those snows my looks shall be soft-going.

Fair-copied according to the MS on 18 October 1917, the poem is addressed to Arthur Newboult, the seven-year-old son of Edinburgh friends, the subject also of the sonnet, No. 130, 'Sweet is your antique body, not yet young' (p. 129) (WO, 229–30).

> 1 Cp. WO to SO, 18 October 1917: 'Yesterday I did go to Newboults – an event you will no doubt hear of. Chubby Cubby had grown, and his face altered. But the old gold and olive ensheath him as in Summer.' (CL, 501)

MSS, p. 254

99 SIX O'CLOCK IN PRINCES STREET

In twos and threes, they have not far to roam,
    Crowds that thread eastward, gay of eyes;
Those seek no further than their quiet home,
    Wives, walking westward, slow and wise.

5 Neither should I go fooling over clouds,
    Following gleams unsafe, untrue,
And tiring after beauty through star-crowds,
    Dared I go side by side with you;

Or be you in the gutter where you stand,
10   Pale rain-flawed phantom of the place,
With news of all the nations in your hand,
    And all their sorrows in your face.

Written at Craiglockhart sometime between August and October 1917 (WO, 124). On 8 August 1917, WO told SO: 'At present I am a sick man in hospital, by night; a poet, for quarter of an hour after breakfast; I am whatever and whoever I see while going down to Edinburgh on the tram: greengrocer, policeman, shopping lady, errand boy, paper-boy, blind man, crippled Tommy, bank-clerk, carter, all of these in half an hour; next a German student in earnest; then I either peer over bookstalls in back-streets, or do a bit of a dash down Princes Street, – according as I have taken weak tea or strong coffee for breakfast' (CL, 480–1).

    TITLE Princes Street is one of the main streets of Edinburgh.
    4 wives, walking westward: Gillian Nelson calls attention to this and other echoes in the poem of Wordsworth, 'Stepping Westward'.
    6 Cp. Tennyson, 'Merlin and the Gleam', ll. 7–10,
      I am Merlin,
      And *I* am dying,
      I am Merlin
      Who follow The Gleam.
    WO parodied these lines in his letter of 27 November 1917 to SS: 'I am Owen; and I am dying. / I am Wilfred; and I follow the Gleam' (CL, 512).
    7 Cp. Yeats, 'When you are old', l. 12, 'And hid his face amid a crowd of stars.'
    10–12 Graham Holliday has pointed out the similarity between these lines and Cowper's description of the postman in *The Task*, IV. 5–7:

THE ONE REMAINS

I sometimes think of those pale, perfect faces
My wonder has not looked upon, as yet;
And of those others never to be met;
And often pore I on the secret traces
5 Left in my heart, of countenances seen,
And lost as soon as seen, – but which mine eye
Remembers as my old home, or the lie
Of landscapes whereupon my windows lean.

And as for those long known and worshipped long,
10 But now, alas! no longer, and the song
Of voices that have said 'Adieu, we part,'
Their reminiscences would cease my heart,
Except I still hoped find, some time, some place,
All beauty, once for ever, in one face.

Revised either at Craiglockhart in October–November 1917, or at Scarborough between November 1917 and January 1918, having been drafted some time earlier.

TITLE Taken from Shelley, *Adonais*, l. 459: 'The One remains, the many change and pass.'

MSS, p. 256

---

       the herald of a noisy world,
With spatter'd boots, strapp'd waist, and frozen locks,
News from all nations lumb'ring at his back.

12 Cp. Yeats, 'When you are old', l. 8, 'And loved the sorrows of your changing face.'

MSS, p. 255

101 THE SLEEPING BEAUTY

Sojourning through a southern realm in youth,
I came upon a house by happy chance
Where bode a marvellous Beauty. There, romance
Flew faerily until I lit on truth –
5 For lo! the fair Child slumbered. Though, forsooth,
She lay not blanketed in drowsy trance,
But leapt alert of limb and keen of glance,
From sun to shower; from gaiety to ruth;
Yet breathed her loveliness asleep in her:
10 For, when I kissed, her eyelids knew no stir.
So back I drew tiptoe from that Princess,
Because it was too soon, and not my part,
To start voluptuous pulses in her heart,
And kiss her to the world of Consciousness.

Written at Bagnères sometime between August and October 1914 (WO, 106–7), and revised either at Craiglockhart in October–November 1917, or at Scarborough between November 1917 and January 1918.

    2 house: The Villa Lorenzo, home of the Léger family.
    3 Beauty: Nénette Léger.

MSS, p. 258

The city lights along the waterside
Kindled serene as blessèd candleshine.
The fires of western heaven, far and wide,
Rose like the reredos of a mighty shrine.
Slow swung the odorous trees from side to side,
Like censers, twining twilight mist for fume;
And on the mountain, that high altar-tomb,
The sun stood full of wine, blood-sanctified.

Soft, soft as angels mounting starry stairs
The smoke upclomb to space; the while a wind
Sung like an organ voicing many prayers.
I, sliding beads, mine errors to rescind,
Of slowly slipping tears, heard God, who cares,
Ineffable God, give pardon that I sinned.

Revised either at Craiglockhart in October–November 1917, or at Scarborough between November 1917 and January 1918, having been drafted some time earlier.

MS, p. 260

103 AUTUMNAL

If it be very strange and sorrowful
To scent the first night-frost in autumntide;
If on the moaning eve when Summer died
Men shuddered, awed to hear her burial;
And if the dissolution of one rose
(Whereof the future holds unnumbered store)
Engender human tears, – ah! how much more
Sorrows and suffers he whose sense foreknows
The weakening and the withering of a love,
The dying of a love that had been dear!
Who feels upon a hand, but late love-warm,
A hardness of indifference, like a glove;
And in the dead calm of a voice may hear
The menace of a drear and mighty storm.

Revised either at Craiglockhart in October–November 1917, or at Scarborough between November 1917 and January 1918, having been drafted some time earlier.

MSS, p. 261

THE UNRETURNING

Suddenly night crushed out the day and hurled
Her remnants over cloud-peaks, thunder-walled.
Then fell a stillness such as harks appalled
When far-gone dead return upon the world.

5 There watched I for the Dead; but no ghost woke.
Each one whom Life exiled I named and called.
But they were all too far, or dumbed, or thralled,
And never one fared back to me or spoke.

Then peered the indefinite unshapen dawn
10 With vacant gloaming, sad as half-lit minds,
The weak-limned hour when sick men's sighs are drained.
And while I wondered on their being withdrawn,
Gagged by the smothering Wing which none unbinds,
I dreaded even a heaven with doors so chained.

Drafted in late 1912 or early 1913, this sonnet was revised either at Craiglockhart in October–November 1917, or at Scarborough between November 1917 and January 1918. On the back of the earliest sheet of rough working, WO drafted a letter to the vicar of Dunsden setting out his objections to 'The Christian Life' (wo, 85–6).

  TITLE Cp. No. 85, 'Happiness' (p. 88), l. 12: 'The former happiness is unreturning.'

    5–8 Cp. Harold Munro, 'God', ll. 25–7:
> for when the daylight broke,
> And rapturously I called upon his name,
> He was not there, He neither heard nor spoke.

      6 Cp. Verlaine, 'Mon Rêve familier', l. 11: 'Comme ceux des aimés que la Vie exila'. WO made an autograph copy of this poem.

    11 Cp. Sir Lewis Morris, *The Epic of Hades* (1879), 'Andromeda', ll. 137–8: 'the dead dark hour before the dawn / When sick men die'. WO quoted from these lines in his letter of January 1912 to MO: 'you know that at 3 a.m. our life ebbs at its lowest; that is "the hour when sick men die" ' (CL, 106).

MSS, p. 262

105 PERVERSITY

    We all love more the Passed and the To Be
    Than actual time, and far things more than near.
    Perverse we all are somehow; calling dear
    Rather the rare than fair. But as for me,
5 How singular and sad that I should see
    More loveliness in Grecian marbles clear
    Than modern flesh, to beauty insincere;
    Less glory in a man than any tree.

    I fall in love with children, elfin fair;
10 Portraits; dark ladies in dark tales antique;
    Or instantaneous faces passed in streets.
    I know the dim old gods that never were,
    Better than men. One friend I love unique,
    But now, thou canst not dream I love thee, Keats!

Revised either at Craiglockhart in October–November 1917, or at Scarborough between November 1917 and January 1918, having been drafted some time earlier.

    3 Cp. Keats, 'Lamia', II. 69–70: 'He thereat was stung, / Perverse'.
    6 Cp. Keats, Fragment of 'The Castle Builder', ll. 59–61:
        That I should rather love a Gothic waste
        Of eyesight on cinque-coloured potter's clay,
        Than on the marble fairness of old Greece.
    9 Cp. Keats, 'La Belle Dame sans Merci', l. 29: 'elfin grot'.

MSS, p. 264

MAUNDY THURSDAY

Between the brown hands of a server-lad
The silver cross was offered to be kissed.
The men came up, lugubrious, but not sad,
And knelt reluctantly, half-prejudiced.
(And kissing, kissed the emblem of a creed.)
Then mourning women knelt; meek mouths they had,
(And kissed the Body of the Christ indeed.)
Young children came, with eager lips and glad.
(These kissed a silver doll, immensely bright.)
Then I, too, knelt before that acolyte.
Above the crucifix I bent my head:
The Christ was thin, and cold, and very dead:
And yet I bowed, yea, kissed – my lips did cling.
(I kissed the warm live hand that held the thing.)

Probably drafted at Shrewsbury in May/June 1915 (WO, 119–20), a recollection of 'the Veneration of the Cross', a Roman Catholic rite in which WO may have participated at Mérignac on Good Friday (not Maundy Thursday) 1914 with the de la Touche family. This dating is supported by a passage in his letter of 27 December 1914 to SO: 'We made two journeys to church with the bath chair, and installed both the boys and ourselves in the very sanctuary. An interesting position for me, all mixed up with the candles, incense, acolytes, chasuble and such like. . . . I think the efforts of the dear, darling little acolytes to keep awake was what took most of my attention there'. (CL, 311) The poem was revised either at Craiglockhart in October–November 1917, or at Scarborough between November 1917 and January 1918.

MS, p. 265

107 THE PERIL OF LOVE

As men who call on spirits get response
And woo successfully the coy Unseen,
Deeming the thing amusement for the nonce,
But later, when dark spirits intervene
5 Uncalled, perceive how an invading mind,
Not to be shaken off, compels them serve
Mad promptings; poisons love of life and kind;
Drains force; clogs brain; and flusters nerve:

So I, lightly addressing me to love,
10 Have found too late love's grave significance.
A fierce infatuation, far above
The zeal for fame or fortune, like a trance,
Exhausts my faculties. I am a prey
Of impulse, the marasmus of decay.

Revised either at Craiglockhart in October–November 1917, or at Scarborough between November 1917 and January 1918, having been drafted some time earlier.

14 marasmus: progressive emaciation.

MSS, p. 265

THE POET IN PAIN

Some men sing songs of Pain and scarcely guess
Their import, for they never knew her stress.
And there be other souls that ever lie
Begnawed by seven devils, silent. Aye,
Whose hearts have wept out blood, who not once spake
Of tears. If therefore my remorseless ache
Be needful to proof-test upon my flesh
The thoughts I think, and in words bleeding-fresh
Teach me for speechless sufferers to plain,
I would not quench it. Rather be my part
To write of health with shaking hands, bone-pale,
Of pleasure, having hell in every vein,
Than chant of care from out a careless heart,
To music of the world's eternal wail.

Revised either at Craiglockhart in October–November 1917, or at Scarborough between November 1917 and January 1918, having been drafted some time earlier.

9 plain: mourn, complain.

MS, p. 265

109

Whither is passed the softly-vanished day?
It is not lost by seeming spent for aye.
For as no bar of incense fumeth out
But leaveth finer perfume all about,
So the sweet hours, though fast they waste away,
In mild Moneta's shrine like odours stray,
And steal on us as, entering there, devout,
We shut the door upon the world without.

And likewise, too, the souls of men are freed.
Sweet lives in their consuming sweeter grow,
And larger, and more wholly earth-released.
Not prayer, unfired and faint, the high gods heed,
But the spent essence of a life aglow
Perfumeth heaven with fragrance unsurceased.

Drafted at Shrewsbury, probably in 1911–12, and revised either at Craiglockhart in October–November 1917, or at Scarborough between November 1917 and January 1918.

1 Cp. Keats, 'To Autumn', l. 25: 'the soft-dying day'.
6 Moneta: The 'majestic shadow' (her Latin name suggests 'the Admonisher') who, in Keats's 'The Fall of Hyperion', replaces the figure of Mnemosyne – goddess of Memory – who appears to him in the earlier 'Hyperion'.

MSS, p. 266

ON MY SONGS

Though unseen Poets, many and many a time,
Have answered me as if they knew my woe,
And it might seem have fashioned so their rime
To be my own soul's cry; easing the flow
Of my dumb tears with language sweet as sobs,
Yet are there days when all these hoards of thought
Hold nothing for me. Not one verse that throbs
Throbs with my heart, or as my brain is fraught.

'Tis then I voice mine own weird reveries:
Low croonings of a motherless child, in gloom
Singing his frightened self to sleep, are these.
One night, if thou shouldst lie in this Sick Room,
Dreading the Dark thou darest not illume,
Listen; my voice may haply lend thee ease.

Drafted at Dunsden on 4 January 1913 (CL, 175), under the influence of James Russell Lowell's sonnet, 'To the Spirit of Keats', quoted in WO's letter to SO of 17 September 1912:
  'Great soul, thou sittest with me in my room,
  Uplifting me with thy vast quiet eyes,
  On whose full orbs with kindly lustre, lies
  The twilight warmth of ruddy ember-gloom.
  Thy clear strong tones will oft bring sudden bloom
  Of hope secure to him who lonely cries,
  Wrestling with the young poet's agonies,
  Neglect and scorn, which seem a certain doom.'   (CL, 160)
WO revised his sonnet either at Craiglockhart in October–November 1917, or at Scarborough between November 1917 and January 1918.

MSS, p. 266

III TO ——

    Three rompers run together, hand in hand.
    The middle boy stops short, the others hurtle:
    What bumps, what shrieks, what laughter turning turtle.
    Love, racing between us two, has planned
5 A sudden mischief: shortly he will stand
    And we shall shock. We cannot help but fall;
    What matter? Why, it will not hurt at all,
    Our youth is supple, and the world is sand.

    Better our lips should bruise our eyes, than He,
10 Rude Love, out-run our breath; you pant, and I,
    I cannot run much farther, mind that we
    Both laugh with Love; and having tumbled, try
    To go forever children, hand in hand.
    The sea is rising . . . and the world is sand.

Drafted in London on 10 May 1916 (WO, **138**), this sonnet is almost certainly a recollection of a day with the de la Touche boys. WO to SO, 23 July 1915: 'I shall part with the four boys with regret, – with three of them regretfully, with two of them sorrowfully, and with one of them very sorrowfully indeed' (CL, 348). The dedicatory title was written in pencil on the one MS, probably later than the poem and with Johnny de la Touche in mind. The sonnet was revised either at Craiglockhart in October–November 1917, or at Scarborough between November 1917 and January 1918.

MS, p. 268

TO EROS

In that I loved you, Love, I worshipped you;
In that I worshipped well, I sacrificed.
All of most worth I bound and burnt and slew:
The innocent small things, fair friends and Christ.

5 I slew all falser loves, I slew all true,
For truth is the prime lie men tell a boy.
Glory I cast away, as bridegrooms do
Their splendid garments in their haste of joy.

But when I fell and held your sandalled feet,
10 You laughed; you loosed away my lips; you rose.
I heard the singing of your wings' retreat;
And watched you, far-flown, flush the Olympian snows,
Beyond my hoping. Starkly I returned
To stare upon the ash of all I burned.

Revised either at Craiglockhart in October–November 1917, or at Scarborough between November 1917 and January 1918, this sonnet was probably drafted some time earlier. It appears to relate to the crisis of WO's last days at Dunsden (WO, 84–5).

TITLE Eros, the Greek god of Love.
  5 Cp. WO to SO, 4 January 1913: 'Murder will out, and I have murdered my false creed. If a true one exists, I shall find it. If not, adieu to the still falser creeds that hold the hearts of nearly all my fellow men.' (CL, 175)
  12 The ancient Greeks believed the summit of Mount Olympus to be the home of the gods.
  14 Cp. WO to SO, 30 July 1917: 'I saw better the supremer beauty of the ashes of all your Sacrifices' (CL, 479).

MSS, p. 269

1914

War broke: and now the Winter of the world
With perishing great darkness closes in.
The foul tornado, centred at Berlin,
Is over all the width of Europe whirled,
5 Rending the sails of progress. Rent or furled
Are all Art's ensigns. Verse wails. Now begin
Famines of thought and feeling. Love's wine's thin.
The grain of human Autumn rots, down-hurled.

For after Spring had bloomed in early Greece,
10 And Summer blazed her glory out with Rome,
An Autumn softly fell, a harvest home,
A slow grand age, and rich with all increase.
But now, for us, wild Winter, and the need
Of sowings for new Spring, and blood for seed.

Drafted in France in late 1914 (WO, 105), and revised either at Craiglockhart in October–November 1917, or at Scarborough between November 1917 and January 1918.

  1 Cp. Shelley, *The Revolt of Islam*, IX. 25: 'This is the winter of the world; – and here / We die.' WO wrote to SO, 18 March 1916: 'Now is the winter of the world. But my life has come already to its month of March.' (CL, 386)

  7 The apparent echo of Rupert Brooke's 'red / Sweet wine of youth' is probably fortuitous. His sonnet 'The Dead' was not published until December 1914, and one draft of '1914' is dated 1914.

  8 Cp. the later MS draft of No. 150, 'Asleep' (p. 152), l. 18: 'And finished fields of autumns that are old' (MSS, p. 314).

  9 Cp. Keats, 'To Autumn', ll. 23–5:
    Where are the songs of Spring? Aye, where are they?
      Think not of them, thou hast thy music too –
    While barred clouds bloom the soft-dying day.

12 Cp. Shakespeare, Sonnet 97, l. 6: 'The teeming autumn big with rich increase'.

MSS, p. 270

PURPLE

Vividly gloomy, with bright darkling glows
Of nebulae and warm, night-shimmering shores!
Stain of full fruits, wines, passions, and the cores
Of all quick hearts! Yet from its deeps there blows
5 Aroma and romance of violets;
Softness of far land, hazed; pacific lift
Of smoke through quiet trees; and that wild drift
Of smoulder when the flare of evening sets.

Solemn, columnar, thunder-throning cloud
10 Wears it so stately that therein the King
Stands before men, and lies in death's hand, proud.
Purest, it is the diamond dawn of spring;
And yet the veil of Venus, whose rose skin,
Mauve-marbled, purples Eros' mouth for sacred sin.

Drafted, according to a dated MS, in September 1916, this poem may have been the first to be prepared on a 'subject' agreed by WO, ELG, and their mutual friend Olwen Joergens (WO, 161–3). For a fuller account of these competitive compositions, see DH, '"Rival Pieces on a Chosen Theme": 'A Note on Some of Wilfred Owen's Minor Poems', *Four Decades of Poetry 1890–1930* (Merseyside), i, no. 1 (January 1976), 70–5. Since purple was WO's favourite colour, he may have chosen this subject. ELG's poem 'Purple' appeared in *The Nymph and Other Poems* (1917). WO's sonnet was revised either at Craiglockhart in October–November 1917, or at Scarborough between November 1917 and January 1918.

>6 pacific: Cp. No. 65, 'A Palinode' (p. 77), l. 45, and No. 92, 'I know the music' (p. 485): 'pacific lamentations'.

MSS, p. 271

115 ON A DREAM

    I leaned, blank-eyed, in lonely thoughtless thought,
    Upon the night, athwart my threshold stone;
    When there came One with hurried, frightened moan,
    With tear-drained eyes, wild hair, and hands distraught,
5   Who fell about my knees, and swift besought
    Help and my love, for she was all alone
    For love of me; and from her world out-thrown.
    I knew that lovely head; her hands I caught;

    For hours I felt her lips warm on my cheek,
10 As through the vast void of the dark we fled.
    For precious hours her limbs in mine were curled,
    Until with utter joy I tried to speak:
    And lo! I raved with fever on my bed,
    And melancholy dawn bestirred the world.

Revised either at Craiglockhart in October–November 1917, or at Scarborough between November 1917 and January 1918, this sonnet was probably drafted some time earlier. Dream and poem clearly owe something to Keats, 'La Belle Dame sans Merci', and Verlaine, 'Mon Rêve familier'.

MS, p. 273

Stunned by their life's explosion into love   I
Some men stay deaf and dizzy ever after,
And blindly through the press they grope or shove,
Nor heed they more of sorrowing or laughter.

5   And others, having fixed their hope above,
Chastened and maimed by bitter chastity,
Grow to forget spring flowers, and why the dove
Makes music with her fellow, endlessly.

Ah! pity these were told not that their thirsts
10 Are slaked nor by priest's wine nor lust's outbursts,
But Poesy. They, knowing Verse to be
God's soothest answer to all passion's plea,
And loving beauties writ and wrought of art,
Might yet have kept a whole and splendid heart.

Revised either at Craiglockhart in October–November 1917, or at Scarborough between November 1917 and January 1918, having been drafted some time earlier.

12 soothest: truest.

MSS, p. 274

117 FROM MY DIARY, JULY 1914

    Leaves
        Murmuring by myriads in the shimmering trees.
    Lives
        Wakening with wonder in the Pyrenees.
5   Birds
        Cheerily chirping in the early day.
    Bards
        Singing of summer, scything through the hay.
    Bees
10 Shaking the heavy dews from bloom and frond.
    Boys
        Bursting the surface of the ebony pond.
    Flashes
        Of swimmers carving through the sparkling cold.
15 Fleshes
        Gleaming with wetness to the morning gold.
    A mead
        Bordered about with warbling waterbrooks.
    A maid
20 Laughing the love-laugh with me; proud of looks.
    The heat
        Throbbing between the upland and the peak.
    Her heart
        Quivering with passion to my pressèd cheek.
25 Braiding
        Of floating flames across the mountain brow.
    Brooding
        Of stillness; and a sighing of the bough.
    Stirs
30 Of leaflets in the gloom; soft petal-showers;
    Stars
        Expanding with the starr'd nocturnal flowers.

Drafted either at Craiglockhart in October–November 1917, or at Scarborough between November 1917 and January 1918, this early exercise in pararhyme is a recollection of days at the Villa Lorenzo, outside Bagnères-de-Bigorre in the French Pyrenees (WO, 106, 211). In fact, WO did not reach Bagnères-de-Bigorre until 31 July 1914, but presumably he dates his 'diary'

THE BALLAD OF MANY THORNS

A Poet stood in parley
   With Carls a-reaping corn.
Quoth one: 'I curse the Barley,
   More sharp than any thorn.'

'Although thy hand be torn,
   Ill-spoken was thy curse:
I swear thou art forsworn,
   If Thistle wound not worse.'

So groaned a footsore Climber,
   Had scaled the bristly path:
'What thorns, Sir Carl, Sir Rimer,
   Like these the Thistle hath?'

Behold a wan youth ramble
   With bleeding cheeks forlorn,
And moans: 'The wanton bramble,
   It is the keenest thorn.'

Rode by a wounded Warrior
   Deep muttering like a lion:
'Show me the flesh wound sorrier
   Than by the barb of Iron!'

Out laughed a man of folly,
   Much wine had made him thick:
'The jolly, festive Holly
   Deals oft a nasty prick.'

---

entry July, rather than August, to suggest the last days of peace. The poem has elements in common with No. 86, 'Songs of Songs' (p. 89), and No. 64, 'Impromptu/Now, let me feel' (p. 76).

   3–4 These lines have been cancelled in the MS.
   19 A maid: Probably Nénette Léger.

MS, p. 275

25   There hung near by a Jesus
         With crownèd head for scorn.
     'Ah by His brow, who sees us,
         Was any like His thorn?'

     So sighed a leprous Palmer.
30   But when he thought afresh:
     'Perchance His pain was calmer,
         Than this thorn in my flesh.'

     Then cried the gentle Poet:
         'Not one among ye knows:
35   The cruelest thorn, I know it,
         For having kissed the Rose.'

Written or revised at Craiglockhart in October–November 1917, or at Scarborough between November 1917 and January 1918.

    4   Cp. Anon., 'The Holly and the Ivy': 'The holly bears a prickle / As sharp as any thorn.'

35–6   Probably an allusion to Albertina Marie Dauthieu, the nineteen-year-old daughter of the publican of The Thistle public house in Milnathort, a village near Edinburgh. WO wrote in her autograph book a gallant adaptation of a song from the opera *Merrie England*, ending:
    And so I'll have my posy
    Of the fairest flower that blows
    Embower'd by the Thistle
    And accompanied by a Rose.
              (WO, 231)

MS, p. 277

I saw his round mouth's crimson deepen as it fell,
    Like a sun, in his last deep hour;
Watched the magnificent recession of farewell,
    Clouding, half gleam, half glower,
And a last splendour burn the heavens of his cheek.
    And in his eyes
The cold stars lighting, very old and bleak,
    In different skies.

Drafted, probably at Scarborough, in November–December 1917, this poem, or fragmentary poem, may be a development of No. 121, 'Spells and Incantation' (p. 494).

    7–8 Cp. Yeats, 'A Dream of Death', l. 9: 'And left her to the indifferent stars above.'

MS, p. 277

123 APOLOGIA PRO POEMATE MEO

I, too, saw God through mud, –
   The mud that cracked on cheeks when wretches smiled.
   War brought more glory to their eyes than blood,
   And gave their laughs more glee than shakes a child.

Merry it was to laugh there –
   Where death becomes absurd and life absurder.
   For power was on us as we slashed bones bare
   Not to feel sickness or remorse of murder.

I, too, have dropped off Fear –
   Behind the barrage, dead as my platoon,
   And sailed my spirit surging light and clear
   Past the entanglement where hopes lay strewn;

And witnessed exultation –
   Faces that used to curse me, scowl for scowl,
   Shine and lift up with passion of oblation,
   Seraphic for an hour; though they were foul.

I have made fellowships –
   Untold of happy lovers in old song.
   For love is not the binding of fair lips
   With the soft silk of eyes that look and long,

By Joy, whose ribbon slips, –
   But wound with war's hard wire whose stakes are strong;
   Bound with the bandage of the arm that drips;
   Knit in the webbing of the rifle-thong.

I have perceived much beauty
   In the hoarse oaths that kept our courage straight;
   Heard music in the silentness of duty;
   Found peace where shell-storms spouted reddest spate.

Nevertheless, except you share
   With them in hell the sorrowful dark of hell,
   Whose world is but the trembling of a flare
   And heaven but as the highway for a shell,

You shall not hear their mirth:
You shall not come to think them well content
35 By any jest of mine. These men are worth
Your tears. You are not worth their merriment.

Written at Scarborough in November–December 1917 (WO, **250**–2). The final fair copy is dated 'Nov. 1917', but it is tempting to see the poem as a response to a remark in Robert Graves's letter *circa* 22 December 1917: 'For God's sake cheer up and write more optimistically – The war's not ended yet but a poet should have a spirit above wars' (CL, 596). Graves may have said much the same to WO earlier.

TITLE   SS corrected the faulty Latin grammar of WO's own title, 'Apologia pro Poema Mea', which may have been influenced by that of Cardinal Newman's *Apologia Pro Vita Sua*.

1   too: Welland, 67–8, argues convincingly that this is an allusion to Graves's poem 'Two Fusiliers':

And have we done with War at last?	By all the misery and loud sound,
Well, we've been lucky devils both,	By a Spring day,
And there's no need of pledge or oath	By Picard clay.
To bind our lovely friendship fast,	
By firmer stuff	Show me the two so closely bound
Close bound enough.	As we, by the wet bond of blood,
	By friendship, blossoming from mud,
By wire and wood and stake we're bound,	By Death: we faced him, and we found
By Fricourt and by Festubert,	Beauty in Death,
By whipping rain, by the sun's glare,	In dead men breath.

13   exultation: Cp. Shelley, 'A Defence of Poetry': 'Poetry is a mirror which makes beautiful that which is distorted. . . . it exalts the beauty of that which is most beautiful, and it adds beauty to that which is most deformed; it marries exultation and horror.'

18–20   Cp. ELG, 'L'Amour', published in *The Nymph and Other Poems* (November 1917), ll. 1–2: 'Love is the binding of souls together, / The binding of lips, the binding of eyes.'

21   Cp. Keats, 'Ode on Melancholy', l. 22: 'And Joy, whose hand is ever at his lips'.

MSS, p. 278

LE CHRISTIANISME

So the church Christ was hit and buried
   Under its rubbish and its rubble.
In cellars, packed-up saints lie serried,
   Well out of hearing of our trouble.

One Virgin still immaculate
   Smiles on for war to flatter her.
She's halo'd with an old tin hat,
   But a piece of hell will batter her.

Written, probably at Scarborough, in late November or early December 1917. At the foot of the corrected fair copy WO has written 'Quivières', a village where he was quartered in April 1917 (WO, **183**), but as Quivières has no church, his memory may have been at fault.

  1 Cp. No. 137, 'At a Cavalry near the Ancre' (p. 134), ll. 1–2.
  4 Cp. A. E. Housman, 'On Wenlock edge the wood's in trouble', ll. 19–20: 'Today the Roman and his trouble / Are ashes under Uricon.'
  8 A pun may be intended, 'piece' meaning both fragment and field-gun, as opposed to 'the peace of God'.

MS, p. 281

HOSPITAL BARGE

Budging the sluggard ripples of the Somme,
A barge round old Cérisy slowly slewed.
Softly her engines down the current screwed,
And chuckled softly with contented hum,
5 Till fairy tinklings struck their croonings dumb.
The waters rumpling at the stern subdued;
The lock-gate took her bulging amplitude;
Gently from out the gurgling lock she swum.

One reading by that calm bank shaded eyes
10 To watch her lessening westward quietly.
Then, as she neared the bend, her funnel screamed.
And that long lamentation made him wise
How unto Avalon, in agony,
Kings passed in the dark barge which Merlin dreamed.

Written at Scarborough in December 1917, following 'a Saturday night revel in "The Passing of Arthur"' (EB, 124; see also WO, 248–9). On 10 May 1917, WO had written to SO: 'I sailed in a steam-tug about 6 miles down the Canal with another "inmate". The heat of the afternoon was Augustan; and it has probably added another year to my old age to have been able to escape marching in equipment under such a sun. The scenery was such as I never saw or dreamed of since I read the *Fairie Queene*. Just as in the Winter when I woke up lying on the burning cold snow I fancied I must have died & been pitch-forked into the Wrong Place, so, yesterday, it was not more difficult to imagine that my dusky barge was wending up to Avalon, and the peace of Arthur, and where Lancelot heals him of his grievous wound. But the Saxon is not broken, as we could very well hear last night. Later, a real thunderstorm did its best to seem terrible, and quite failed.' (CL, 457)

TITLE Cérisy is one and a half miles down the Somme Canal from Gailly where WO was a patient in the 13th Casualty Clearing Station.

9 reading: The poem implies that the speaker was reading Malory, *Morte Darthur*, or a later retelling such as Tennyson, 'The Passing of Arthur', from *The Holy Grail and Other Poems* (1870). WO bought a copy of the latter book in Edinburgh in July 1917.

12 lamentation: Cp. Tennyson, 'The Passing of Arthur', ll. 361–71:
  Then saw they how there hove a dusky barge,
  Dark as a funeral scarf from stem to stern,
  Beneath them; and descending they were ware
  That all the decks were dense with stately forms,

>   Black-stoled, black-hooded, like a dream – by these
>   Three Queens with crowns of gold: and from them rose
>   A cry that shivered to the tingling stars,
>   And, as it were one voice, an agony
>   Of lamentation, like a wind that shrills
>   All night in a waste land, where no one comes,
>   Or hath come, since the making of the world.

14 In November 1917 WO had marked in his copy of Alfred Austin, *Songs of England* (1898), 'The Passing of Merlin', V:

>   A wailing cometh from the shores that veil
>   Avilion's island valley; on the mere,
>   Looms through the mist and wet winds weeping blear
>   A dusky barge, which, without oar or sail,
>   Fades to the far-off fields where falls nor snow nor hail.

MSS, p. 281

Sweet is your antique body, not yet young.
Beauty withheld from youth that looks for youth.
Fair only for your father. Dear among
Masters in art. To all men else uncouth
Save me; who know your smile comes very old,
Learnt of the happy dead that laughed with gods;
For earlier suns than ours have lent you gold,
Sly fauns and trees have given you jigs and nods.

But soon your heart, hot-beating like a bird's,
Shall slow down. Youth shall lop your hair,
And you must learn wry meanings in our words.
Your smile shall dull, because too keen aware;
And when for hopes your hand shall be uncurled,
Your eyes shall close, being opened to the world.

Written at Craiglockhart, probably (given the diction shared with No. 139, 'Miners') in December 1917. The child addressed in this sonnet is Arthur Newboult, the seven-year-old son of Edinburgh friends (WO, 230). In its theme and phrasing, the poem shows the influence of Wordsworth's ode, 'Intimations of Immortality from Recollections of Early Childhood'.

    8 fauns (WO wrote 'fawns'): Cp. 'Miners' (p. 135), l. 8.
   11 wry: Cp. 'Miners', l. 15.

MSS, p. 284

133 PAGE EGLANTINE

Nay, light me no fire tonight,
    Page Eglantine;
I have no desire tonight
    To drink or dine;
5 I will suck no briar tonight,
    Nor read no line;
An you be my quire tonight,
    And you my wine.

Written at Scarborough between November 1917 and February 1918, 'Page Eglantine' may be related to the 'privie page' of No. 84, 'Ballad of Lady Yolande' (p. 472).

    5 briar: briar pipe.
    7 quire: archaic variant of 'choir'.

MS, p. 284

THE RIME OF THE YOUTHFUL MARINER

One knotted a rope with an evil knout,
    And flogged me till I fell;
And he is picking the rope end out
    In a land-locked prison-cell.

5 One tied my wrist with a twisted cord
    While I lay asleep on deck.
But his reward was overboard,
    With the string around his neck.

One bound my mouth with her hands of silk,
10   And drew me backward so.
Her skin that was foul as curdled milk
    Is fouler today, I trow.

One clogged my feet with a heavy wine,
    And my tongue with a tangling drug.
15 But now his tongue is thicker than mine
    And black as any slug.

One bound my thighs with his muscled arm,
    Whose weight was good to bear.
O may he come to no worse harm
20   Than what he wrought me there.

Written at Scarborough between November 1917 and January 1918.

TITLE Cp. Coleridge, *The Rime of the Ancient Mariner*.
    1 knout: A whip for flogging criminals, but incorrectly used by WO as a variant form of 'knot'. Cp. No. 163, 'Mental Cases' (p. 169), l. 26: 'Picking at the rope-knouts of their scourging'.
    3 picking the rope end out: The picking of oakum (loose fibres from old hemp ropes, subsequently used for caulking the seams of ships) was once a common form of employment for prisoners.

MS, p. 285

135   *Who is the god of Canongate?*
           I, for I trifle with men and fate.

   Art thou high in the heart of London?
           Yea, for I do what is done and undone.

5 *What is thy throne, thou barefoot god?*
           All pavements where my feet have trod.

   Where is thy shrine, then, little god?
           Up secret stairs men mount unshod.

   Say what libation such men fill?
10   There lift their lusts and let them spill.

   Why do you smell of the moss in Arden?
           If I told you, Sir, your look would harden.

   What are you called, I ask your pardon?
           I am called the Flower of Covent Garden.

15 *What shall I pay for you, lily-lad?*
           Not all the gold King Solomon had.

   How can I buy you, London Flower?
           Buy me for ever, but not for an hour.

   When shall I pay you, Violet Eyes?
20   With laughter first, and after with sighs.

   But you will fade, my delicate bud?
           No, there is too much sap in my blood.

   Will you not shrink in my shut room?
           No, there I'll break into fullest bloom.

Written, probably at Scarborough, between November 1917 and February 1918 (WO, **240–1**).

MY SHY HAND

My shy hand shades a hermitage apart, –
   O large enough for thee, and thy brief hours.
Life there is sweeter held than in God's heart,
   Stiller than in the heavens of hollow flowers.

5 The wine is gladder there than in gold bowls.
   And Time shall not drain thence, nor trouble spill.
Sources between my fingers feed all souls,
   Where thou mayest cool thy lips, and draw thy fill.

Five cushions hath my hand, for reveries;
10   And one deep pillow for thy brow's fatigues;
Languor of June all winterlong, and ease
   For ever from the vain untravelled leagues.

Thither your years may gather in from storm,
And Love, that sleepeth there, will keep thee warm.

Drafted at Craiglockhart in August 1917 and revised at Scarborough in January–February 1918, this sonnet shows the influence of Yeats's 'To an Isle in the Water' (wo, **212–13**).

MSS, p. 286

---

1 and 14 Canongate and Covent Garden are districts of Edinburgh and
      London, respectively.

MSS, p. 285

137 AT A CALVARY NEAR THE ANCRE

One ever hangs where shelled roads part.
  In this war He too lost a limb,
But His disciples hide apart;
  And now the Soldiers bear with Him.

5 Near Golgotha strolls many a priest,
  And in their faces there is pride
That they were flesh-marked by the Beast
  By whom the gentle Christ's denied.

The scribes on all the people shove
10   And bawl allegiance to the state,
But they who love the greater love
  Lay down their life; they do not hate.

Written probably in late 1917 or early 1918, WO having been involved in fighting near the river Ancre in January 1917 (CL, 421 n.). DH's note is to the point: 'As in [No. 166] "The Parable of the Old Man and the Young", WO adapts Biblical detail to fit the war. In the Gospel story, the *Soldiers* kept watch at the cross while Christ's *disciples* hid in fear of the authorities; *priests* and *scribes* passed by in scorn. The Church sends priests to the trenches, where they watch the common soldier being, as it were, crucified, and they take pride in minor wounds (*flesh-marked*, l. 7) as a sign of their opposition to Germany (*the Beast*). *Flesh-marked*, however, carries a further meaning: the Devil used to be believed to leave his finger-marks on the flesh of his followers (cf. Revelation 14: 9–10). Thus the Church's hatred of Germany (l. 12) puts it in the Devil's following; and the priests' wounds are signs not so much of opposition to the Devil Germany as of allegiance to the Devil War. Christ said "Love one another" *and* "Love your enemies"; despite the exhortations of Church and State, WO perceives that "pure Christianity will not fit in with pure patriotism" [CL, 461].' (DH, 116)

  TITLE Calvary or Golgotha (both words meaning 'the place of the skull', from Lat. *calvaria* and Heb. *gulgōleth* respectively) was the site of the Crucifixion. A Calvary is a model of the crucified Christ, such as is found at many crossroads in France.

  4 Two senses of 'bear with' seem intended: 'humour' and 'carry the cross with'.

  11–12 John 15: 13: 'Greater love hath no man than this, that a man lay down his life for his friends.' See also No. 161, 'Greater Love' (p. 166).

MS, p. 287

MINERS

There was a whispering in my hearth,
    A sigh of the coal,
Grown wistful of a former earth
    It might recall.

I listened for a tale of leaves
    And smothered ferns,
Frond-forests, and the low sly lives
    Before the fauns.

My fire might show steam-phantoms simmer
    From Time's old cauldron,
Before the birds made nests in summer,
    Or men had children.

But the coals were murmuring of their mine,
    And moans down there
Of boys that slept wry sleep, and men
    Writhing for air.

And I saw white bones in the cinder-shard,
    Bones without number.
Many the muscled bodies charred,
    And few remember.

I thought of all that worked dark pits
    Of war, and died
Digging the rock where Death reputes
    Peace lies indeed.

Comforted years will sit soft-chaired,
    In rooms of amber;
The years will stretch their hands, well-cheered
    By our life's ember;

The centuries will burn rich loads
    With which we groaned,
Whose warmth shall lull their dreaming lids,

>   While songs are crooned;
> But they will not dream of us poor lads,
>   Left in the ground.

Written at Scarborough on 13 or 14 January 1918 (WO, 253–7). On 12 January a pit explosion at the Podmore Hall Colliery, Halmerend, killed about 140 men and boy miners. WO presumably read the newspaper accounts, that in the *Daily News* of 14 January being headlined 'Colliery Disaster', and the same day he told SO: 'Wrote a poem on the Colliery Disaster: but I get mixed up with the War at the end. It is short, but oh! sour.' (EB, 125) He showed it to SS, who proposed alterations which, with questionable judgement, WO would seem to have accepted (see p. 287). On 17 January he sent his mother 'the Coal Poem' and two days later wrote to her: 'With your beautiful letter came a proof from the *Nation* of my "Miners". This is the first poem I have sent to the *Nation* myself, and it has evidently been accepted. It was scrawled out on the back of a note to the Editor; and no penny stamp or addressed envelope was enclosed for return! That's the way to do it. "Miners" will probably appear next Saturday [26 January].' It did, and that evening WO wrote to ELG: 'You may feel keen enough to buy this week's *Nation*. I have at last a poem in it, which I sent off on the same evening as writing!!.' This produced 'blunt criticism' from ELG, whose 'musical ear' was offended by his cousin's rhymes, and on 12 February WO replied: 'I suppose I am doing in poetry what the advanced composers are doing in music. I am not satisfied with either. Still I am satisfied with the Two Guineas that half-hour's work brought me. Got the Cheque this m'ng!' (CL, 527–31)

DH ('Wilfred Owen and the Georgians', RES, n.s., xxx, no. 117 [1979], 28–40) has detected the influence of the introductory poem in W. W. Gibson's *Fires* (1912). Gibson sees pleasant pictures in the embers, including forests:

>   Till, dazzled by the drowsy glare,
>   I shut my eyes to heat and light;
>   And saw, in sudden night,
>   Crouched in the dripping dark,
>   With steaming shoulders stark,
>   The man who hews the coal to feed my fire.

In 'Miners', the watcher by the hearth expects the coal to tell of its prehistoric origin – WO was an amateur geologist – but instead it speaks of the sufferings of miners, in whom WO had been interested (WO, 76–8, 136–7, 230) long before he commanded a platoon containing several in 1916. The Halmerend disaster prompts a vision of the fate of such miners and those others who dug perilous 'saps' under No Man's Land to mine the enemy lines. At the poem's end WO sees himself sharing their common trench, mine, grave, hell. See Jennifer Breen, 'The Dating and Sources of Wilfred Owen's "Miners"', N&Q, n.s., xxi, no. 10 [October 1974], 366–70, and William Cooke, 'Wilfred Owen's "Miners" and the Minnie Pit Disaster', *English*, xxvi, no. 126 (Autumn 1977), 213–17.

>   8 fauns (WO wrote 'fawns'): Cp. No. 130, 'Sweet is your antique body, not yet young' (p. 129), l. 8.

THE LETTER

With B.E.F. June 10. Dear Wife,
(Oh blast this pencil. 'Ere, Bill, lend's a knife.)
I'm in the pink at present, dear.
I think the war will end this year.
5   We don't see much of them square-'eaded 'Uns.
We're out of harm's way, not bad fed.
I'm longing for a taste of your old buns.
(Say, Jimmie, spare's a bite of bread.)
There don't seem much to say just now.
10 (Yer what? Then don't, yer ruddy cow!
And give us back me cigarette!)
I'll soon be 'ome. You mustn't fret.
My feet's improvin', as I told you of.
We're out in rest now. Never fear.
15 (VRACH! By crumbs, but that was near.)
Mother might spare you half a sov.
Kiss Nell and Bert. When me and you –
(Eh? What the 'ell! Stand to? Stand to!
Jim, give's a hand with pack on, lad.
20 Guh! Christ! I'm hit. Take 'old. Aye, bad.
No, damn your iodine. Jim? 'Ere!
Write my old girl, Jim, there's a dear.)

Written, probably at Scarborough but possibly at Ripon, between January and March 1918.

   1 B.E.F.: British Expeditionary Force.
   3 in the pink: in very good health.
  18 Stand to: Abbreviated form of the command 'Stand to arms', meaning 'Prepare for/to attack'.

MS, p. 288

  19 Previous editors read 'For many hearts with coal are charred', an interlinear suggestion added to the MS by SS. I prefer WO's original line.
  24 lies: A pun would be in keeping with the tone of the poem.
  34 Previous editors read 'Lost in the ground', an interlinear suggestion added to the MS by SS. I prefer WO's original verb.

MS, p. 287

142 CONSCIOUS

His fingers wake, and flutter; up the bed.
His eyes come open with a pull of will,
Helped by the yellow mayflowers by his head.
The blind-cord drawls across the window-sill . . .
5   What a smooth floor the ward has! What a rug!
Who is that talking somewhere out of sight?
Three flies are creeping round the shiny jug . . .
'Nurse! Doctor!' – 'Yes, all right, all right.'

But sudden evening blurs and fogs the air.
10   There seems no time to want a drink of water.
Nurse looks so far away. And here and there
Music and roses burst through crimson slaughter.
He can't remember where he saw blue sky . . .
The trench is narrower. Cold, he's cold; yet hot –
15   And there's no light to see the voices by . . .
There is no time to ask . . . he knows not what.

Written, probably at Scarborough but possibly at Ripon, between January and March 1918, this poem shows the influence of SS, 'The Death-Bed' (WO, 256).

3 Cp. WO to MO from 13th Casualty Clearing Station, 8 May 1917: 'Meanwhile I have superb weather, sociably-possible friends, great blue bowls of yellow Mayflower, baths and bed *ad lib*' (CL, 456).

9 Cp. WO to SO, 14 August 1912: 'sudden twilight seemed to fall upon the world' (CL, 153).

10 Cp. SS, 'The Death-Bed', l. 7: 'Someone was holding water to his mouth.'

12 Cp. SS, 'The Death-Bed', l. 9: 'Through crimson gloom to darkness'.

MSS, p. 288

SCHOOLMISTRESS

Having, with bold Horatius, stamped her feet
And waved a final swashing arabesque
O'er the brave days of old, she ceased to bleat,
Slapped her Macaulay back upon the desk,
5   Resumed her calm gaze and her lofty seat.

There, while she heard the classic lines repeat,
Once more the teacher's face clenched stern;
For through the window, looking on the street,
Three soldiers hailed her. She made no return.
10 One was called 'Orace whom she would not greet.

Written, probably at Scarborough but possibly at Ripon, between January and March 1918, this poem may derive from WO's experience at the Tynecastle Secondary School, Edinburgh, where he gave English lessons in September–October 1917 (WO, 215).

TITLE EB and CDL entitle this poem 'Bold Horatius'.
  1 The schoolmistress has been reading Thomas Babington Macaulay's poem 'Hòratius' from *Lays of Ancient Rome*.

MSS, p. 290

144 DULCE ET DECORUM EST

Bent double, like old beggars under sacks,
Knock-kneed, coughing like hags, we cursed through sludge,
Till on the haunting flares we turned our backs
And towards our distant rest began to trudge.
5 Men marched asleep. Many had lost their boots
But limped on, blood-shod. All went lame; all blind;
Drunk with fatigue; deaf even to the hoots
Of tired, outstripped Five-Nines that dropped behind.

Gas! G<small>AS</small>! Quick, boys! – An ecstasy of fumbling,
10 Fitting the clumsy helmets just in time;
But someone still was yelling out and stumbling,
And flound'ring like a man in fire or lime . . .
Dim, through the misty panes and thick green light,
As under a green sea, I saw him drowning.

15 In all my dreams, before my helpless sight,
He plunges at me, guttering, choking, drowning.

If in some smothering dreams you too could pace
Behind the wagon that we flung him in,
And watch the white eyes writhing in his face,
20 His hanging face, like a devil's sick of sin;
If you could hear, at every jolt, the blood
Come gargling from the froth-corrupted lungs,
Obscene as cancer, bitter as the cud
Of vile, incurable sores on innocent tongues, –
25 My friend, you would not tell with such high zest
To children ardent for some desperate glory,
The old Lie: Dulce et decorum est
Pro patria mori.

Drafted at Craiglockhart in the first half of October 1917 (WO, 226–8), this poem was revised, probably at Scarborough but possibly at Ripon, between January and March 1918. The earliest surviving MS is dated 'Oct. 8. 1917', and on the [? 16th] WO wrote to SO: 'Here is a gas poem, done yesterday, (which is not private, but not final). The famous Latin tag [from Horace, *Odes*, III. ii. 13] means of course It is sweet and meet to die for one's country. Sweet! and decorous!' (CL, 499–500)

    5 Men . . . Many: Cp. WO to SO, 16 January 1917: '. . . craters full of water. Men have been known to drown in them. Many stuck in the mud . . .' (CL, 427)

    8 WO never finalized this line (see MS on p. 292). Five-Nines: 5.9-calibre shells.

    9 GAS: Cp. WO to SO, 19 January 1917: 'I went on ahead to scout – foolishly alone – and when, half a mile away from the party, got overtaken by GAS' (CL, 428).

  12 flound'ring: 'I remember [WO] using this word floundering and, unable to resist the play, adding, " . . . but of course there is, I suppose, the possibility you might founder" ' (JFO, III. 132).

  13 panes: The gas mask's celluloid windows.

17–25 you . . . My friend: Jessie Pope, to whom the poem was originally to have been dedicated, was the author of numerous pre-war children's books, as well as of *Jessie Pope's War Poems* (1915), *More War Poems* (1915), and *Simple Rhymes for Stirring Times* (1916) (WO, 227).

MSS, p. 292

145 A TEAR SONG

    Out of the endless nave
        Chorus tremendous,
    While the gruff organ gave
        Sponses stupendous.

5   But of a surety
        Not one among them
    Said the psalms heartfully
        Of all that sung them,

    Saving one chorister,
10   Sweet as gay bugles when
    Robin the Forester
        Rallied his merry men.

    Opened his little teeth
        Like the round daisy's.
15   Smiled they for things beneath,
        Or Zion's praises?

    He sang of friendly bees
        Not of the hills that skip,
    It was that morning's breeze
20   Piped on his lip.

    But his eyes jewelled were
        Of his own singing,
    God saw the sparkle there
        On his lids clinging.

25   God the boy's jewel took
        Into His casket,
    Flinging the anthem book
        On His waste-basket.

      God for his glittering world
30   Seeketh our tears.
      Prayers show as eyelids pearled.
          God hath no ears.

Drafted, probably at Scarborough, between November 1917 and January 1918, and revised between January and March.

  25–6 Cp. Keats, 'Isabella', liv: 'So that the jewel, safely casketed, / Came forth'.

MSS, p. 298

146 THE DEAD-BEAT

      He dropped, – more sullenly than wearily,
      Lay stupid like a cod, heavy like meat,
      And none of us could kick him to his feet;
      – Just blinked at my revolver, blearily;
5   – Didn't appear to know a war was on,
      Or see the blasted trench at which he stared.
      'I'll do 'em in,' he whined. 'If this hand's spared,
      I'll murder them, I will.'

                    A low voice said,
      'It's Blighty, p'raps, he sees; his pluck's all gone,
10 Dreaming of all the valiant, that *aren't* dead:
      Bold uncles, smiling ministerially;
      Maybe his brave young wife, getting her fun
      In some new home, improved materially.
      It's not these stiffs have crazed him; nor the Hun.'

15 We sent him down at last, out of the way.
      Unwounded; – stout lad, too, before that strafe.
      Malingering? Stretcher-bearers winked, 'Not half!'

      Next day I heard the Doc's well-whiskied laugh:
      'That scum you sent last night soon died. Hooray!'

Begun on 22 August 1917, when WO wrote to ELG: 'At last I have an event worth a letter. I have beknown myself to Siegfried Sassoon. Went in to him last night (my second call). . . . After leaving him, I wrote something in Sassoon's style, which I may as well send you, since you ask for the latest.' A fair copy of 'The Dead-Beat' followed, and the next day WO continued his letter: '. . . He was struck with the "Dead Beat", but pointed out that the facetious bit was out of keeping with the first & last stanzas. Thus the piece as a whole is no good.' (CL, 485–6) WO salvaged – and probably adapted – eight lines of 'the facetious bit' for his editorial in *The Hydra*, no. 10 (1 September 1917). The poem was revised at Ripon between March and May 1918.

    9 Blighty: soldiers' slang for 'Britain'.
   16 strafe: artillery bombardment (from the German phrase, *Gott strafe England*, meaning 'God punish England').

MSS, p. 298

INSENSIBILITY

1
Happy are men who yet before they are killed
Can let their veins run cold.
Whom no compassion fleers
Or makes their feet
Sore on the alleys cobbled with their brothers.
The front line withers.
But they are troops who fade, not flowers,
For poets' tearful fooling:
Men, gaps for filling:
Losses, who might have fought
Longer; but no one bothers.

2
And some cease feeling
Even themselves or for themselves.
Dullness best solves
The tease and doubt of shelling,
And Chance's strange arithmetic
Comes simpler than the reckoning of their shilling.
They keep no check on armies' decimation.

3
Happy are these who lose imagination:
They have enough to carry with ammunition.
Their spirit drags no pack.
Their old wounds, save with cold, can not more ache.
Having seen all things red,
Their eyes are rid
Of the hurt of the colour of blood for ever.
And terror's first constriction over,
Their hearts remain small-drawn.
Their senses in some scorching cautery of battle
Now long since ironed,
Can laugh among the dying, unconcerned.

4
Happy the soldier home, with not a notion
How somewhere, every dawn, some men attack,

And many sighs are drained.
Happy the lad whose mind was never trained:
His days are worth forgetting more than not.
He sings along the march
Which we march taciturn, because of dusk,
The long, forlorn, relentless trend
From larger day to huger night.

5

We wise, who with a thought besmirch
Blood over all our soul,
How should we see our task
But through his blunt and lashless eyes?
Alive, he is not vital overmuch;
Dying, not mortal overmuch;
Nor sad, nor proud,
Nor curious at all.
He cannot tell
Old men's placidity from his.

6

But cursed are dullards whom no cannon stuns,
That they should be as stones.
Wretched are they, and mean
With paucity that never was simplicity.
By choice they made themselves immune
To pity and whatever moans in man
Before the last sea and the hapless stars;
Whatever mourns when many leave these shores;
Whatever shares
The eternal reciprocity of tears.

Drafted either at Craiglockhart in October–November 1917, or at Scarborough between November 1917 and January 1918, this Pindaric ode – perhaps a reply to Wordsworth's 'Character of the Happy Warrior' (WO, 261) – may have been revised at Ripon in April 1918. WO wrote to ELG on 21 April: 'In my Chaumbers under the roof of a cottage (7 Borage Lane, Ripon) I have written, I think, two poems: one an Ode which, considering my tuneless tendencies, may be called dam good, excuse me' (CL, 546–7). However, DH argues persuasively (in a letter to the editor) that WO is here referring to his 'Elegy in April and September' (No. 173), which in its April version was entitled 'Ode for a Poet' and given musical annotations (see p. 184).

TITLE Cp. Shelley, 'A Defence of Poetry': 'It [Poetry] is as it were the interpenetration of a diviner nature through our own; but its footsteps are like those of a wind over a sea, which the coming calm erases, and those traces remain only, as on the wrinkled sand which paves it. These and corresponding conditions of being are experienced principally by those of the most delicate sensibility and the most enlarged imagination; and the state of mind produced by them is at war with every base desire.'

1 Cp. Wordsworth, 'Character of the Happy Warrior', ll. 1–2: 'Who is the happy Warrior? Who is he / That every man in arms should wish to be?'

5 cobbled with their brothers: Cp. WO to MO, ? 25 March 1918: 'They are dying again at Beaumont Hamel, which already in 1916 was cobbled with skulls' (CL, 542).

8 fooling: Cp. No. 99, 'Six O'clock in Princes Street' (p. 102), l. 5: 'Neither should I go fooling over clouds.'

9 gaps for filling: DH notes that 'The gaps had been illustrated on a number of recruiting posters. "Fill up the Ranks!" was a familiar slogan; one poster shows a long line of men in which a single empty space is filled by a billboard marked "This space is Reserved for a Fit Man". The repeated use of the word "happy" in the . . . poem, to describe the soldier who has been rendered "insensible to war" by war experience, is reminiscent of another poster which shows a smiling Tommy and the caption, "He's happy and satisfied / Are You?".' ('Some Contemporary Allusions in Poems by Rosenberg, Owen and Sassoon', N&Q, n.s., xxvi, no. 4 [August 1979], 333)

17 shilling: The 'King's shilling' was that traditionally given to the newly enlisted soldier by the recruiting officer.

19 imagination: Cp. Shelley, 'A Defence of Poetry', quoted above.

40 We wise: we poets.

55 moans: SS, CDL, and DH (but see DH, 125) read 'mourns'. WO, however, clearly cancelled 'mourns' and wrote 'moans' above it. See p. 301

56 Cp. Tennyson, 'Oenone', l. 215: 'Between the loud stream and the trembling stars'.

59 reciprocity: Cp. John Drinkwater, 'Reciprocity', a poem printed in *The Hydra*, New Series, no. 1, 2. There is a MS among WO's papers.

MSS, p. 301

148 STRANGE MEETING

It seemed that out of battle I escaped
Down some profound dull tunnel, long since scooped
Through granites which titanic wars had groined.

Yet also there encumbered sleepers groaned,
Too fast in thought or death to be bestirred.
Then, as I probed them, one sprang up, and stared
With piteous recognition in fixed eyes,
Lifting distressful hands, as if to bless.
And by his smile, I knew that sullen hall, –
By his dead smile I knew we stood in Hell.

With a thousand pains that vision's face was grained;
Yet no blood reached there from the upper ground,
And no guns thumped, or down the flues made moan.
'Strange friend,' I said, 'here is no cause to mourn.'
'None,' said that other, 'save the undone years,
The hopelessness. Whatever hope is yours,
Was my life also; I went hunting wild
After the wildest beauty in the world,
Which lies not calm in eyes, or braided hair,
But mocks the steady running of the hour,
And if it grieves, grieves richlier than here.
For by my glee might many men have laughed,
And of my weeping something had been left,
Which must die now. I mean the truth untold,
The pity of war, the pity war distilled.
Now men will go content with what we spoiled,
Or, discontent, boil bloody, and be spilled.
They will be swift with swiftness of the tigress.
None will break ranks, though nations trek from progress.
Courage was mine, and I had mystery,
Wisdom was mine, and I had mastery:
To miss the march of this retreating world
Into vain citadels that are not walled.
Then, when much blood had clogged their chariot-wheels,
I would go up and wash them from sweet wells,
Even with truths that lie too deep for taint.

I would have poured my spirit without stint
But not through wounds; not on the cess of war.
Foreheads of men have bled where no wounds were.

40 'I am the enemy you killed, my friend.
I knew you in this dark: for so you frowned
Yesterday through me as you jabbed and killed.
I parried; but my hands were loath and cold.
Let us sleep now. . . .'

Drafted, probably at Scarborough but possibly at Ripon, between January and March 1918, this poem may be a development of the fragment, No. 120, 'With those that are become' (p. 492), drafted in November 1917. Certainly, it incorporates another fragment, No. 131, 'Earth's wheels run oiled with blood' (p. 514), written between November 1917 and January 1918. For a full and illuminating discussion of the interplay of echoes in 'Strange Meeting' from the Bible, Barbusse, Cary's translation of Dante, Keats, Shelley, Sir Lewis Morris, Harold Monro, and SS, see Bäckman, 96–117. The MSS suggest that WO may not have regarded the poem as complete.

TITLE Welland was the first to cp. Shelley, *The Revolt of Islam*, ll. 1828–32:
    And one whose spear had pierced me, leaned beside,
      With quivering lips and humid eyes; – and all
    Seemed like some brothers on a journey wide
      Gone forth, whom now strange meeting did befall
      In a strange land. . . .
Cp. also Harold Monro, *Strange Meetings* (1917).

2 tunnel: Cp. SS, 'The Rear-Guard', ll. 1–3:
    Groping along the tunnel, step by step,
    He winked his prying torch with patching glare
    From side to side, and sniffed the unwholesome air.
Bäckman suggests the influence of a childhood memory of a nightmare walk down an 'immensely long and dark' drive, roofed with trees 'so that the effect was of a rather dark tunnel' (JFO, I. 80).
scooped: Cp. Shelley, *The Revolt of Islam*, ll. 2913–15:
    He plunged through the green silence of the main,
      Through many a cavern which the eternal flood
      Had scooped, as dark lairs for its monster brood. . . .
Also *Alastor*, ll. 423–5:
                 There, huge caves,
    Scooped in the dark base of their aëry rocks
    Mocking its moans, respond and roar for ever.

3 granites: Cp. WO to SO, 18 ? February 1917: 'the men had to dig trenches in ground like granite' (CL, 436).

4 encumbered: Cp. WO to SO, 1 February 1916: 'When I was going up the subway at Liverpool St. from the Underground to the Gt. Eastern Platform, I noticed the passages unduly encumbered, and found the outlet just closed' (CL, 377).

6–11 Cp. the poet's vision of Moneta's face, 'bright-blanched / By an immortal sickness which kills not' in Keats, 'The Fall of Hyperion'; also Dante, *Hell* (in the 1805 translation by the Revd Henry Francis Cary, a copy of which WO possessed), XV. 22–9:

    I was agnized of one, who by the skirt
Caught me, and cried, 'What wonder have we here?'
And I, when he to me outstretch'd his arm,
    Intently fix'd my ken on his parch'd looks,
That, although smirch'd with fire, they hinder'd not
But I remember'd him; and towards his face
    My hand inclining, answer'd, 'Ser Brunetto!
And are ye here?'

25 Cp. WO's Preface (p. 535): 'My subject is War, and the pity of War. The Poetry is in the pity.'

28 Cp. II Samuel 1: 23: 'Saul and Jonathan were lovely and pleasant in their lives, and in their death they were not divided: they were swifter than eagles, they were stronger than lions.'

29 Presumably an allusion to the Great Trek of the South African Boer farmers in 1835–6.

32 Cp. No. 83, 'The Fates' (p. 87), l. 14: 'And miss the march of lifetime, stage by stage.'

34 chariot-wheels: Cp. Shelley, *Queen Mab*, VII. 33–5:
                whether hosts
Stain his death-blushing chariot-wheels, as on
Triumphantly they roll, ...

36 Cp. Wordsworth, Ode on 'Intimations of Immortality from Recollections of Early Childhood', l. 205: 'Thoughts that do often lie too deep for tears'.

39 Cp. Luke 22: 44: 'and his sweat was as it were great drops of blood falling to the ground.'

40 Cp. Oscar Wilde, 'The Ballad of Reading Gaol', l. 37: 'Yet each man kills the thing he loves.' This line, misquoted, appears in the fragment, No. 120, 'With those that are become' (p. 492). Cp. also Henri Barbusse, *Under Fire* (1917), 288: 'When I'm sleeping I dream that I'm killing him over again!'

44 Cp. No. 26, 'Science has looked and sees no life but this' (p. 36): 'Let me but sleep . . .', and No. 126, 'The Women and the Slain' (p. 502): 'Keep silent. Let us sleep' (line cancelled).

MSS, p. 306

SONNET

On Seeing a Piece of Our Heavy Artillery
Brought into Action

Be slowly lifted up, thou long black arm,
Great Gun towering towards Heaven, about to curse;
Sway steep against them, and for years rehearse
Huge imprecations like a blasting charm!
Reach at that Arrogance which needs thy harm,
And beat it down before its sins grow worse.
Spend our resentment, cannon, – yea, disburse
Our gold in shapes of flame, our breaths in storm.

Yet, for men's sakes whom thy vast malison
Must wither innocent of enmity,
Be not withdrawn, dark arm, thy spoilure done,
Safe to the bosom of our prosperity.
But when thy spell be cast complete and whole,
May God curse thee, and cut thee from our soul!

Revised at Scarborough in May 1918, but perhaps begun as early as July 1917.

9 malison: malediction, curse.

MS, p. 311

ASLEEP

Under his helmet, up against his pack,
After so many days of work and waking,
Sleep took him by the brow and laid him back.

There, in the happy no-time of his sleeping,
5   Death took him by the heart. There heaved a quaking
Of the aborted life within him leaping,
Then chest and sleepy arms once more fell slack.

And soon the slow, stray blood came creeping
From the intruding lead, like ants on track.

10 Whether his deeper sleep lie shaded by the shaking
Of great wings, and the thoughts that hung the stars,
High-pillowed on calm pillows of God's making,
Above these clouds, these rains, these sleets of lead,
And these winds' scimitars,
15 – Or whether yet his thin and sodden head
Confuses more and more with the low mould,
His hair being one with the grey grass
Of finished fields, and wire-scrags rusty-old,
Who knows? Who hopes? Who troubles? Let it pass!
20 He sleeps. He sleeps less tremulous, less cold,
Than we who wake, and waking say Alas!

Written, probably in Shrewsbury, on 14 November 1917 (WO, 237–8) and revised at Ripon the following May. On 16 November 1917, WO wrote to ELG: 'Good of you to send me the Lyric of Nov. 14th. I can only send my own of the same date, which came from Winchester Downs, as I crossed the long backs of the downs after leaving you. It is written as from the trenches. I could almost see the dead lying about in the hollows of the downs.' (CL, 508) The subject of the poem suggests an acquaintance with Rimbaud's 'Le dormeur du val'. DH argues persuasively for the influence of Robert Graves's *Fairies and Fusiliers* (1917), which WO bought on the day he began 'Asleep' ('Wilfred Owen and the

Georgians', RES, n.s., xxx, no. 117 [1979], 36); and Bäckman detects and discusses (40–2) an important debt to Milton's 'Lycidas'. Previous editors follow an earlier version.

>   1–9 Cp. Swinburne, 'Laus Veneris', ll. 1–4:
>   Asleep or waking is it? for her neck,
>   Kissed over close, wears yet a purple speck
>   Wherein the pained blood falters and goes out;
>   Soft, and stung softly – fairer for a fleck.
>   17 Cp. WO to SO, 24 May 1914: 'It was curious you asked about my grey hairs, for just last week I noticed they were cropping up again. In winter they died down, with the grass.' (CL, 252)

MSS, p. 312

151 ARMS AND THE BOY

    Let the boy try along this bayonet-blade
    How cold steel is, and keen with hunger of blood;
    Blue with all malice, like a madman's flash;
    And thinly drawn with famishing for flesh.

5   Lend him to stroke these blind, blunt bullet-leads,
    Which long to nuzzle in the hearts of lads,
    Or give him cartridges whose fine zinc teeth
    Are sharp with sharpness of grief and death.

    For his teeth seem for laughing round an apple.
10 There lurk no claws behind his fingers supple;
    And God will grow no talons at his heels,
    Nor antlers through the thickness of his curls.

Written, or at any rate fair-copied, at 7 Borrage Lane, Ripon, on 3 May 1918, this poem was classified by WO in his draft list of contents (Appendix B) under 'Protest – the unnaturalness of weapons'.

  TITLE Cp. SS, 'Arms and the Man' and Harold Monro, 'Youth in Arms'.
    1–4 Cp. Shelley, *The Mask of Anarchy*, lxxvii. ll. 311–14:
        Let the fixèd bayonet
        Gleam with sharp desire to wet
        Its bright point in English blood
        Looking keen as one for food.
      6 Paul Fussell observes that 'Bret Harte's "What the Bullet Sang", one of the few American poems available in the *Oxford Book [of English Verse*, edited by Sir Arthur Quiller-Couch], seems to lie behind both Sassoon's "The Kiss" and Owen's "Arms and the Boy", both of which, like Harte's poem, make much of the quasi-erotic desire of the bullet (and in Sassoon, the bayonet) to "kiss" or "nuzzle" the body of its adolescent target.' (*The Great War and Modern Memory* [1975], 160)

MSS, p. 315

THE SHOW

> We have fallen in the dreams the ever-living
> Breathe on the tarnished mirror of the world,
> And then smooth out with ivory hands and sigh.
>
> W. B. YEATS

My soul looked down from a vague height, with Death,
As unremembering how I rose or why,
And saw a sad land, weak with sweats of dearth,
Grey, cratered like the moon with hollow woe,
And pitted with great pocks and scabs of plagues.

Across its beard, that horror of harsh wire,
There moved thin caterpillars, slowly uncoiled.
It seemed they pushed themselves to be as plugs
Of ditches, where they writhed and shrivelled, killed.

By them had slimy paths been trailed and scraped
Round myriad warts that might be little hills.

From gloom's last dregs these long-strung creatures crept,
And vanished out of dawn down hidden holes.

(And smell came up from those foul openings
As out of mouths, or deep wounds deepening.)

On dithering feet upgathered, more and more,
Brown strings, towards strings of grey, with bristling spines,
All migrants from green fields, intent on mire.

Those that were grey, of more abundant spawns,
Ramped on the rest and ate them and were eaten.

I saw their bitten backs curve, loop, and straighten.
I watched those agonies curl, lift, and flatten.

Whereat, in terror what that sight might mean,
I reeled and shivered earthward like a feather.

And Death fell with me, like a deepening moan.

And He, picking a manner of worm, which half had hid
Its bruises in the earth, but crawled no further,
Showed me its feet, the feet of many men,
And the fresh-severed head of it, my head.

Drafted at Scarborough in November 1917 and revised at Ripon in May 1918 (WO, **243**–5), this is almost certainly the poem referred to in WO to SS, 27 November 1917: 'My "Vision" is the result of two hours' leisure yesterday, – and getting up early this morning! If you have objections to make, would you return it? If not, pass it on to R[obbie]. R[oss].' (CL, 512) That this 'Vision' was what came to be called 'The Show' (and not the fragment [No. 87, p. 481] 'A Vision in Whitechapel', later retitled 'Lines to a Beauty seen in Limehouse', as the editors of CL suggest) is made clear by WO to SS of 6 December 1917: 'What do you think of my Vowel-rime stunt in this ['Wild with all Regrets', to become No. 168, 'A Terre' (p. 178)], and "Vision"?' (CL, 514)

WO's vision derives from his experience of battlefields between January and May 1917 (see notes to ll, 5 and 26–7 below) and from his reading in November–December 1917 of Henri Barbusse, *Under Fire* (1917). Chapter i of this is entitled 'The Vision':

'The man at the end of the rank cries, "I can see crawling things down there" – "Yes, as though they were alive" – "Some sort of plant perhaps" – "Some kind of men" –

'And there amid the baleful glimmers of the storm, below the dark disorder of the clouds that extend and unfurl over the earth like evil spirits, they seem to see a great livid plain unrolled, which to their seeing is made of mud and water, while figures appear and fast fix themselves to the surface of it, all blinded and borne down with filth, like the dreadful castaways of shipwreck.' (4)

'The Show' may also echo two passages from chapter xx: 'Dwarfed to the size of insects and worms, they make a queer dark stirring among these shadow-hidden and Death-pacified lands . . . (255); and 'In the middle of the plateau and in the depth of the rainy and bitter air, on the ghastly morrow of this debauch of slaughter, there is a head planted in the ground, a wet and bloodless head, with a heavy beard. It is one of ours, and the helmet is beside it.' (265)

TITLE 'Show' was soldiers' slang for 'battle'. Cp. No. 164, 'The Chances' (p. 171), l. 1: 'the night before that show'.

EPIGRAPH WO misquotes Forgael's speech in Yeats's play *The Shadowy Waters (Poems 1899–1905* [1906], 22), which reads 'burnished mirror' (WO, 245). (For WO's ironic use of Yeatsian epigraphs, see Jon Stallworthy, 'W. B. Yeats and Wilfred Owen', *Critical Quarterly*, xi, no. 3 [Autumn 1969], 199–214.)

4–5 Cp. WO to SO, 19 January 1917: '[No Man's Land] is pockmarked like a body of foulest disease and its odour is the breath of cancer. . . . No Man's Land under snow is like the face of the moon chaotic, crater-ridden, uninhabitable, awful, the abode of madness.' (CL, 429)

16–17 The caterpillars 'with bristling spines' are files of soldiers: the Germans in grey uniforms, the British in khaki.

26–7 Cp. WO to CO, 14 May 1917: 'Then we were caught in a Tornado of Shells. The various "waves" were all broken up and we carried on like a crowd moving off a cricket-field. When I looked back and saw the ground all crawling and wormy with wounded bodies, I felt no horror at all but only an immense exultation at having got through the Barrage.' (CL, 458)

29 See the quotation from Barbusse, 265, above. As the commander of a platoon advancing in single file, WO would have been literally and figuratively its 'head'.

MSS, p. 316

153 FUTILITY

    Move him into the sun –
    Gently its touch awoke him once,
    At home, whispering of fields half-sown.
    Always it woke him, even in France,
5   Until this morning and this snow.
    If anything might rouse him now
    The kind old sun will know.

    Think how it wakes the seeds –
    Woke once the clays of a cold star.
10 Are limbs, so dear achieved, are sides
    Full-nerved, still warm, too hard to stir?
    Was it for this the clay grew tall?
    – O what made fatuous sunbeams toil
    To break earth's sleep at all?

Written at Ripon in May 1918.

TITLE Cp. Tennyson, *In Memoriam*, lvi, l. 25: 'O life as futile, then, as frail!' For a discussion of the influence of Tennyson's elegy on WO's, see DH, *Wilfred Owen* (Writers and Their Work, 1975), 32–3.

  3 half-sown: Previous editors read 'unsown'.

  7 old sun: Cp. Donne, 'The Sun Rising', l. 1: 'Busy old fool, unruly sun'.

8–9 Cp. John Davidson, 'Thirty Bob a Week', ll. 71–2: 'A little sleeping seed, I woke – I did, indeed – / A million years before the blooming sun.' Also Sir Walter Scott, Hymn 487, *The English Hymnal*, ll. 9–12:
    O, on that day, that wrathful day,
    When man to judgement wakes from clay,
    Be thou the trembling sinner's stay,
    Though heaven and earth shall pass away!

MSS, p. 319

THE END

After the blast of lightning from the east,
  The flourish of loud clouds, the Chariot Throne;
After the drums of time have rolled and ceased,
  And by the bronze west long retreat is blown,
Shall Life renew these bodies? Of a truth,
  All death will he annul, all tears assuage?
Or fill these void veins full again with youth,
  And wash, with an immortal water, age?

When I do ask white Age, he saith not so:
  'My head hangs weighed with snow.'
And when I hearken to the Earth, she saith:
  'My fiery heart shrinks, aching. It is death.
Mine ancient scars shall not be glorified,
  Nor my titanic tears, the seas, be dried.'

Begun probably in late 1916; continued either at Craiglockhart in October–November 1917, or at Scarborough between November 1917 and January 1918; this poem is almost certainly that referred to in WO's letter of 12 February 1917 to SO: 'Leslie tells me that Miss Joergens considers my Sonnet on "The End" the finest of the lot. Naturally, because it is, intentionally, in her style!' (CL, 434). No. 112, 'To Eros' (p. 115), was also, at one time, entitled 'The End', as was the unfinished fragment, No. 119, on p. 491. ELG's 'The End' was published in *YM / The British Empire YMCA Weekly*, ii, no. 102 (22 December 1916), 1229. DH discusses WO's poem's debt to Shelley, *Prometheus Unbound* (*Wilfred Owen* [Writers and Their Work, 1975], 19–20), and Hilda D. Spear its refutation of the biblical Book of Revelation ('"I Too Saw God": The Religious Allusions in Wilfred Owen's Poetry', *English*, xxiv, no. 119 [Summer 1975], 35–6).

   5–6 Cp. Revelation 21:4, 'And God shall wipe away all tears from their eyes; and there shall be no more death, neither sorrow, nor crying.' For the misquotation from WO's lines on his tombstone, see WO, 288.
   14 titanic tears: Cp. No. 148, 'Strange Meeting' (p. 148), l. 3: 'titanic wars'.

MSS, p. 322

155 S. I. W.

> I will to the King,
> And offer him consolation in his trouble,
> For that man there has set his teeth to die,
> And being one that hates obedience,
> Discipline, and orderliness of life,
> I cannot mourn him.
>
> W. B. YEATS

    I The Prologue
Patting goodbye, doubtless they told the lad
He'd always show the Hun a brave man's face;
Father would sooner him dead than in disgrace, –
Was proud to see him going, aye, and glad.
5 Perhaps his mother whimpered how she'd fret
Until he got a nice safe wound to nurse.
Sisters would wish girls too could shoot, charge, curse . . .
Brothers – would send his favourite cigarette.
Each week, month after month, they wrote the same,
10 Thinking him sheltered in some Y. M. Hut,
Because he said so, writing on his butt
Where once an hour a bullet missed its aim.
And misses teased the hunger of his brain.
His eyes grew old with wincing, and his hand
15 Reckless with ague. Courage leaked, as sand
From the best sandbags after years of rain.
But never leave, wound, fever, trench-foot, shock,
Untrapped the wretch. And death seemed still withheld
For torture of lying machinally shelled,
20 At the pleasure of this world's Powers who'd run amok.

He'd seen men shoot their hands, on night patrol.
Their people never knew. Yet they were vile.
'Death sooner than dishonour, that's the style!'
So Father said.

    II The Action
                One dawn, our wire patrol
25 Carried him. This time, Death had not missed.
We could do nothing but wipe his bleeding cough.
Could it be accident? – Rifles go off . . .
Not sniped? No. (Later they found the English ball.)

III The Poem
It was the reasoned crisis of his soul
30 Against more days of inescapable thrall,
Against infrangibly wired and blind trench wall
Curtained with fire, roofed in with creeping fire,
Slow grazing fire, that would not burn him whole
But kept him for death's promises and scoff,
35 And life's half-promising, and both their riling.

IV The Epilogue
With him they buried the muzzle his teeth had kissed,
And truthfully wrote the mother, 'Tim died smiling.'

Drafted at Craiglockhart in September 1917 and revised at Ripon in May 1918, this poem shows the influence of such poems by SS as 'The Hero' and 'Stand-to: Good Friday Morning'.

TITLE Military abbreviation for 'Self-Inflicted Wound'.
EPIGRAPH From Yeats's play, *The King's Threshold, Poems 1899–1905* (1906), 238. (For WO's ironic use of Yeatsian epigraphs, see Jon Stallworthy, 'W. B. Yeats and Wilfred Owen', *Critical Quarterly*, xi, no. 3 [Autumn 1969], 199–214.)
10 Y. M. Hut: Young Men's Christian Association hostel.
31 blind trench: one with no outlet.
32 creeping fire: A 'creeping barrage' advanced a predetermined distance – usually in front of advancing infantry – at a predetermined time.

MSS, p. 327

157 THE CALLS

A dismal fog-hoarse siren howls at dawn.
I watch the man it calls for, pushed and drawn
Backwards and forwards, helpless as a pawn.
    But I'm lazy, and his work's crazy.

5 Quick treble bells begin at nine o'clock,
Scuttling the schoolboy pulling up his sock,
Scaring the late girl in the inky frock.
    I must be crazy; I learn from the daisy.

Stern bells annoy the rooks and doves at ten.
10 I watch the verger close the doors, and when
I hear the organ moan the first amen,
    Sing my religion's – same as pigeons'.

A blatant bugle tears my afternoons.
Out clump the clumsy Tommies by platoons,
15 Trying to keep in step with rag-time tunes,
    But I sit still; I've done my drill.

Gongs hum and buzz like saucepan-lids at dusk.
I see a food-hog whet his gold-filled tusk
To eat less bread, and more luxurious rusk.

20 Then sometimes late at night my window bumps
From gunnery-practice, till my small heart thumps
And listens for the shell-shrieks and the crumps,
    But that's not all.

For leaning out last midnight on my sill,
25 I heard the sighs of men, that have no skill
To speak of their distress, no, nor the will!
    A voice I know. And this time I must go.

Revised – it may have been written earlier – at Scarborough in May 1918 (WO, 266), and here treated as a poem rather than a fragment – although the manuscript makes clear that its revisions are incomplete – since it has gained currency as such from its appearance in CDL and DH. On 10 August 1918, WO wrote to SO: 'Tomorrow I am for a medical inspection with 21 others, to be declared fit for draft. This means we may be sent on draft leave tomorrow, & I may reach you even before this letter! I know not. I am glad. That is I am much gladder to be going out again than afraid. I shall be better able to cry my outcry, playing my part.' (CL, 568)

18–19 food-hog: Perhaps a reference to 'the stinking Leeds & Bradford War-profiteers' mentioned in the letter to SO quoted above. DH notes that '"Eat less bread" was a widespread slogan in the Food Economy Campaign in 1917. One poster reads, "Save the Wheat / and / Help the Fleet. / Eat / Less / Bread." The Food Controller sent a circular to households in May 1917 and said, "We must all eat less food, especially we must all eat less bread".' ('Some Contemporary Allusions in Poems by Rosenberg, Owen and Sassoon', N&Q, n.s., xxvi, no. 4 [August 1979], 333–4)

19 The MS shows two cancelled attempts at a line following this, and one must suppose that WO intended to try again.

23 Cancelled attempts at this line suggest that WO intended 'But that's not all' to be only its second half.

MS, p. 332

TRAINING

Not this week nor this month dare I lie down
In languor under lime trees or smooth smile.
Love must not kiss my face pale that is brown.

My lips, panting, shall drink space, mile by mile;
5   Strong meats be all my hunger; my renown
Be the clean beauty of speed and pride of style.

Cold winds encountered on the racing Down
Shall thrill my heated bareness; but awhile
None else may meet me till I wear my crown.

Written, probably at Scarborough, in June 1918 (the date on the MS). WO arrived in Scarborough, from Ripon, on 5 June and on 1 July 1918 wrote to SO: 'Went a Cross Country Run last Wednesday, from which my calves are still suffering. Have seldom enjoyed any exercise so much.' (CL, 561)

    4 panting: EB and CDL read 'parting', which also fits the context, but is not, I think, what WO wrote.

    9 Cp. WO to OS, July 1918: 'For 14 hours yesterday I was at work – teaching Christ to lift his cross by numbers, and how to adjust his crown' (CL, 562).

MS, p. 334

THE NEXT WAR

> War's a joke for me and you,
> While we know such dreams are true.
> SIEGFRIED SASSOON

Out there, we walked quite friendly up to Death, –
   Sat down and ate beside him, cool and bland, –
   Pardoned his spilling mess-tins in our hand.
We've sniffed the green thick odour of his breath, –
5 Our eyes wept, but our courage didn't writhe.
   He's spat at us with bullets, and he's coughed
   Shrapnel. We chorused if he sang aloft,
We whistled while he shaved us with his scythe.

Oh, Death was never enemy of ours!
10 We laughed at him, we leagued with him, old chum.
No soldier's paid to kick against His powers.
   We laughed, – knowing that better men would come,
   And greater wars: when every fighter brags
He fights on Death, for lives; not men, for flags.

Written at Craiglockhart in late September 1917 and sent, with No. 96, 'Anthem for Doomed Youth' (p. 99), to SO on the 25th (CL, 496). On 2 October 1917, WO told her: 'I included my "Next War" in order to strike a note. I want Colin to read, mark, learn etc. it.' (CL, 497) The poem was revised at Scarborough in July 1918.

EPIGRAPH SS, 'A Letter Home' (to Robert Graves, written at Flixécourt in May 1916), ll. 73–4.
   14 on: against.

MSS, p. 334

161 GREATER LOVE

Red lips are not so red
    As the stained stones kissed by the English dead.
Kindness of wooed and wooer
Seems shame to their love pure.
5 O Love, your eyes lose lure
    When I behold eyes blinded in my stead!

Your slender attitude
    Trembles not exquisite like limbs knife-skewed,
Rolling and rolling there
10 Where God seems not to care;
Till the fierce love they bear
    Cramps them in death's extreme decrepitude.

Your voice sings not so soft, –
    Though even as wind murmuring through raftered loft, –
15 Your dear voice is not dear,
Gentle, and evening clear,
As theirs whom none now hear,
    Now earth has stopped their piteous mouths that coughed.

Heart, you were never hot
20   Nor large, nor full like hearts made great with shot;
And though your hand be pale,
Paler are all which trail
Your cross through flame and hail:
    Weep, you may weep, for you may touch them not.

Drafted either at Craiglockhart in October–November 1917 (wo, 230–1), or at Scarborough between November 1917 and January 1918, and revised at Scarborough that July, the poem is a response to Swinburne's poem 'Before the Mirror / (Verses Written under a Picture) / Inscribed to J. A. Whistler', ll. 1–7:
    White rose in red rose-garden
        Is not so white;
    Snowdrops that plead for pardon
        And pine for fright
    Because the hard East blows
    Over their maiden rows
        Grow not as this face grows from pale to bright.

WO may also have been aware of Salomé's words to Jokanaan in Wilde's *Salomé*: 'The roses in the garden of the Queen of Arabia are not so white as thy body.' WO had written to SO on 16 [?] May 1917: 'Christ is literally in no man's land. There men often hear His voice: Greater love hath no man than this, that a man lay down his life – for a friend.' (CL, 461)

TITLE   Cp. John 15:13: 'Greater love hath no man than this, that a man lay down his life for his friends.' See also No. 137, 'At a Calvary near the Ancre' (p. 134), ll. 11–12: 'But they who love the greater love / Lay down their life; they do not hate.'

20   Cp. Elizabeth Barrett Browning, *Aurora Leigh*, Second Book, ll. 718–20:
           As my blood recoiled
   From that imputed ignominy, I made
   My heart great with it.
See also WO to SO, 2 April 1916: 'And the drums pulse fearfully-voluptuously, as great hearts in death' (CL, 388).

21   pale: Cp. Swinburne, 'Before the Mirror', quoted above.

22   trail: Used in the military sense of 'trail arms', carry a rifle with butt end near the ground and muzzle pointing forwards.

24   Cp. John 21:15–17: 'Jesus saith unto [Mary Magdalene], Woman, why weepest thou? . . . Jesus saith unto her, Touch me not; for I am not yet ascended to my Father.'

MSS, p. 337

THE LAST LAUGH

'Oh! Jesus Christ! I'm hit,' he said; and died.
Whether he vainly cursed or prayed indeed,
  The Bullets chirped – In vain, vain, vain!
  Machine-guns chuckled – Tut-tut! Tut-tut!
  And the Big Gun guffawed.

Another sighed – 'O Mother, – Mother, – Dad!'
Then smiled at nothing, childlike, being dead.
  And the lofty Shrapnel-cloud
  Leisurely gestured, – Fool!
  And the splinters spat, and tittered.

'My Love!' one moaned. Love-languid seemed his mood,
Till slowly lowered, his whole face kissed the mud.
  And the Bayonets' long teeth grinned;
  Rabbles of Shells hooted and groaned;
  And the Gas hissed.

Drafted at Scarborough in February 1918, an early version of this poem was included in WO's letter of 18 February to SO, and was there prefaced: 'There is a point where prayer is indistinguishable from blasphemy. There is also a point where blasphemy is indistinguishable from prayer. As in this first verse ...' (CL, 534) The first of the three later drafts, in which full rhymes have given place to pararhymes, is dated '5. 3. 18', and WO's subsequent revisions must date from spring–summer 1918 when he gave a final fair copy to OS.

MSS, p. 341

MENTAL CASES

Who are these? Why sit they here in twilight?
Wherefore rock they, purgatorial shadows,
Drooping tongues from jaws that slob their relish,
Baring teeth that leer like skulls' teeth wicked?
Stroke on stroke of pain, – but what slow panic,
Gouged these chasms round their fretted sockets?
Ever from their hair and through their hands' palms
Misery swelters. Surely we have perished
Sleeping, and walk hell; but who these hellish?

– These are men whose minds the Dead have ravished.
Memory fingers in their hair of murders,
Multitudinous murders they once witnessed.
Wading sloughs of flesh these helpless wander,
Treading blood from lungs that had loved laughter.
Always they must see these things and hear them,
Batter of guns and shatter of flying muscles,
Carnage incomparable, and human squander
Rucked too thick for these men's extrication.

Therefore still their eyeballs shrink tormented
Back into their brains, because on their sense
Sunlight seems a blood-smear; night comes blood-black;
Dawn breaks open like a wound that bleeds afresh.
– Thus their heads wear this hilarious, hideous,
Awful falseness of set-smiling corpses.
– Thus their hands are plucking at each other;
Picking at the rope-knouts of their scourging;
Snatching after us who smote them, brother,
Pawing us who dealt them war and madness.

Drafted at Ripon in May 1918 and revised at Scarborough in July, this poem draws on the earlier fragment, No. 70, 'Purgatorial Passions' (p. 455). WO wrote to SO on 25 May: 'I've been "busy" this evening with my terrific poem (at present) called "The Deranged". This poem the Editor of the *Burlington Magazine* – (a 2/6 Arts Journal which takes no poetry) – old More Adey, I say, solemnly prohibited me from sending to the *English Review*, on the grounds that "the *English Review* should not be encouraged".!!!!' (CL, 553) On 15 June 1918 he told SO: 'lo! an urgent request from the Sitwells in London for more of my poems for their 1918 Anthology which is coming out immediately. This is on the strength of "The Deranged", which S. Moncrieff showed them the other day.' (CL, 559) In the event, the Sitwells printed no poems by WO in their anthology *Wheels* (1918).

The poem reflects WO's reading of Dante, and Mr Mark Sinfield points out (in a letter to the editor) that the opening of each stanza echoes the diction and, with bitter irony, parallels the structure of the King James version of Revelation 7:13–17: 'What are these which are arrayed in white robes? and whence came they?... These are they which came out of great tribulation, and have washed their robes, and made them white in the blood of the Lamb. Therefore are they before the throne of God, and serve him day and night in his temple: and he that sitteth on the throne shall dwell among them. They shall hunger no more, neither thirst any more; neither shall the sun light on them, nor any heat. For the Lamb which is in the midst of the throne shall feed them, and shall lead them unto living fountains of waters: and God shall wipe away all tears from their eyes.'

12 Multitudinous murders: Cp. *Macbeth*, II. ii. 58–60:
> No; this my hand will rather
> The multitudinous seas incarnadine,
> Making the green one red.

19 The MS variants of this line confirm the impression that this poem owes something to the influence of Isaac Watts, 'The Day of Judgement', ll. 17–24:

> Hark, the shrill outcries of the guilty wretches!
> Lively bright horror, and amazing anguish,
> Stare thro' their eye-lids, while the living worm lies
>   Gnawing within them.
>
> Thoughts, like old vultures, prey upon their heart-strings,
> And the smart twinges, when the eye beholds the
> Lofty Judge frowning, and a flood of vengeance
>   Rolling afore him.

26 Cp. No. 134, 'The Rime of the Youthful Mariner' (p. 131), ll. 1–3.

MSS, p. 342

THE CHANCES

I 'mind as how the night before that show
Us five got talkin'; we was in the know.
'Ah well,' says Jimmy, and he's seen some scrappin',
'There ain't no more than five things as can happen, –
5   You get knocked out; else wounded, bad or cushy;
Scuppered; or nowt except you're feelin' mushy.'

One of us got the knock-out, blown to chops;
One lad was hurt, like, losin' both his props;
And one – to use the word of hypocrites –
10 Had the misfortune to be took by Fritz.
Now me, I wasn't scratched, praise God Almighty,
Though next time please I'll thank Him for a blighty.
But poor old Jim, he's livin' and he's not;
He reckoned he'd five chances, and he had:
15 He's wounded, killed, and pris'ner, all the lot,
The flamin' lot all rolled in one. Jim's mad.

Drafted at Craiglockhart in August–September 1917, this poem shows the strong influence of SS. It was revised at Scarborough in July 1918.

- 1 show: Soldiers' slang for 'battle'.
- 2 Previous editors follow this line with a couplet omitted from the final version.
- 5 cushy: Soldiers' slang for 'slightly'.
- 6 scuppered: Soldiers' (from nautical) slang for 'killed'.
  nowt: Dialect for 'nothing'.
- 8 props: Soldiers' slang for 'legs'.
- 10 Fritz: Soldiers' slang for 'the Germans'.
- 12 blighty: A wound serious enough to cause a soldier to be sent back to England.

MSS, p. 345

165 THE SEND-OFF

Down the close darkening lanes they sang their way
To the siding-shed,
And lined the train with faces grimly gay.

Their breasts were stuck all white with wreath and spray
As men's are, dead.

Dull porters watched them, and a casual tramp
Stood staring hard,
Sorry to miss them from the upland camp.

Then, unmoved, signals nodded, and a lamp
Winked to the guard.

So secretly, like wrongs hushed-up, they went.
They were not ours:
We never heard to which front these were sent;

Nor there if they yet mock what women meant
Who gave them flowers.

Shall they return to beating of great bells
In wild train-loads?
A few, a few, too few for drums and yells,

May creep back, silent, to village wells,
Up half-known roads.

Drafted at Ripon in April–May 1918 (WO, 261–2), and revised at Scarborough in July, this may be one of the 'two poems' mentioned in WO's letter to ELG of 21 April 1918 (CL, 547). On 4 May he was able to tell SO: 'I have long "waited" for a final stanza to "the Draft" (which begins.

1

"Down the deep, darkening lanes they sang their way
To the waiting train,
And filled its doors with faces grimly gay,
And heads & shoulders white with wreath & spray,
As men's are, slain.")

* * * *

IV

Will they return, to beatings of great bells,
In wild train-loads?
– A few, a few, too few for drums and yells,
May walk back, silent, to their village wells,
Up half-known roads.'   (CL, 550)

6–8 Bäckman observes (43): 'These lines contain a couple of ironic echoes of stanzas 25 and 27 of Gray's "Elegy", where a "hoary-headed swain" is heard to say that he had often seen the departed country poet "brushing with hasty steps the dews away, / To meet the sun upon *the upland lawn*", but then suddenly "one morn", he "*miss'd* him on the custom'd hill". The hoary-headed swain in Gray's lines about the death of an unknown poet becomes "a casual tramp" in Owen's poem commemorating the departure of some soldiers for the front, and Gray's poetic "upland lawn" becomes the more prosaic "upland camp".'

19 Previous editors read 'still village wells'.

MSS, p. 346

THE PARABLE OF THE OLD MAN AND THE YOUNG

So Abram rose, and clave the wood, and went,
And took the fire with him, and a knife.
And as they sojourned both of them together,
Isaac the first-born spake and said, My Father,
Behold the preparations, fire and iron,
But where the lamb, for this burnt-offering?
Then Abram bound the youth with belts and straps,
And builded parapets and trenches there,
And stretchèd forth the knife to slay his son.
When lo! an Angel called him out of heaven,
Saying, Lay not thy hand upon the lad,
Neither do anything to him, thy son.
Behold! Caught in a thicket by its horns,
A Ram. Offer the Ram of Pride instead.

But the old man would not so, but slew his son,
And half the seed of Europe, one by one.

Written, probably at Scarborough, in July 1918, the poem's ll. 1–14 follow the wording of Genesis 22: 1–19 very closely.

7 belts and straps: As of a soldier's equipment.
12–14 Previous editors print an earlier form of these lines.
16 seed: Cp. No. 113, '1914' (p. 116), l. 14: 'blood for seed'.

MSS, p. 350

DISABLED

He sat in a wheeled chair, waiting for dark,
And shivered in his ghastly suit of grey,
Legless, sewn short at elbow. Through the park
Voices of boys rang saddening like a hymn,
Voices of play and pleasure after day,
Till gathering sleep had mothered them from him.

* * *

About this time Town used to swing so gay
When glow-lamps budded in the light blue trees,
And girls glanced lovelier as the air grew dim, –
In the old times, before he threw away his knees.
Now he will never feel again how slim
Girls' waists are, or how warm their subtle hands.
All of them touch him like some queer disease.

* * *

There was an artist silly for his face,
For it was younger than his youth, last year.
Now, he is old; his back will never brace;
He's lost his colour very far from here,
Poured it down shell-holes till the veins ran dry,
And half his lifetime lapsed in the hot race
And leap of purple spurted from his thigh.

* * *

One time he liked a blood-smear down his leg,
After the matches, carried shoulder-high.
It was after football, when he'd drunk a peg,
He thought he'd better join. – He wonders why.
Someone had said he'd look a god in kilts,
That's why; and maybe, too, to please his Meg,
Aye, that was it, to please the giddy jilts
He asked to join. He didn't have to beg;
Smiling they wrote his lie: aged nineteen years.

30   Germans he scarcely thought of; all their guilt,
       And Austria's, did not move him. And no fears
       Of Fear came yet. He thought of jewelled hilts
       For daggers in plaid socks; of smart salutes;
       And care of arms; and leave; and pay arrears;
35   Esprit de corps; and hints for young recruits.
       And soon, he was drafted out with drums and cheers.

        *   *   *

Some cheered him home, but not as crowds cheer Goal.
Only a solemn man who brought him fruits
Thanked him; and then enquired about his soul.

        *   *   *

40   Now, he will spend a few sick years in institutes,
       And do what things the rules consider wise,
       And take whatever pity they may dole.
       Tonight he noticed how the women's eyes
       Passed from him to the strong men that were whole.
45   How cold and late it is! Why don't they come
       And put him into bed? Why don't they come?

Drafted at Craiglockhart in October 1917 (WO, 224–6), and revised at Scarborough in July 1918. On 14 October 1917 WO wrote to SO: 'On Sat. I met Robert Graves. . . . No doubt he thought me a slacker sort of sub. S.S. when they were together showed him my longish war-piece "Disabled" (you haven't seen it) & it seems Graves was mightily impressed, and considers me a kind of <u>Find</u>!! No thanks, Captain Graves! I'll find myself in due time.' (CL, 499) On 18 October he told SO that Graves had 'carried away a Poem, or was carried away with it, without my knowledge. It was only in a <u>Draft</u> State, & I was perfectly aware of all the solecisms.' (CL, 501) A day or two earlier, Graves had written to WO about that 'damn fine poem of yours, that "Disabled"' (CL, 595).

    22 Cp. A. E. Housman, 'To an Athlete Dying Young', ll. 1–4:
        The time you won your town the race
        We chaired you through the market-place;
        Man and boy stood cheering by,
        And home we brought you shoulder-high.
    23 peg: Slang expression for a drink, usually brandy and soda.
    27 jilts: capricious women.

29 they wrote his lie: The recruiting officers entered on his enlistment form his lie that he was nineteen years old and therefore above the minimum age for military service.

45–6 DH calls attention to 'a mocking echo of the slogan on a recruiting poster, probably put out in 1914, which shows soldiers in action and in need of reinforcements. The slogan reads, "Will they never come?". . . .The parallel in this poem between playing football and serving in the Army reflects the recruiting drives that had been made at football matches earlier in the war. The Imperial War Museum preserves the following rather amateur poster: "Men of Millwall / Hundreds of Football enthusiasts / are joining the Army daily. / Don't be left behind. / Let the Enemy hear the 'LION'S ROAR'. Join and be in at THE FINAL / and give them a / KICK OFF THE EARTH".' ('Some Contemporary Allusions in Poems by Rosenberg, Owen and Sassoon', N&Q, n.s., xxvi, no. 4 [August 1979], 333)

MSS, p. 351

168 A TERRE
(being the philosophy of many soldiers)

Sit on the bed. I'm blind, and three parts shell.
Be careful; can't shake hands now; never shall.
Both arms have mutinied against me, – brutes.
My fingers fidget like ten idle brats.

5 I tried to peg out soldierly, – no use!
One dies of war like any old disease.
This bandage feels like pennies on my eyes.
I have my medals? – Discs to make eyes close.
My glorious ribbons? – Ripped from my own back
10 In scarlet shreds. (That's for your poetry book.)

A short life and a merry one, my buck!
We used to say we'd hate to live dead-old, –
Yet now . . . I'd willingly be puffy, bald,
And patriotic. Buffers catch from boys
15 At least the jokes hurled at them. I suppose
Little I'd ever teach a son, but hitting,
Shooting, war, hunting, all the arts of hurting.
Well, that's what I learnt, – that, and making money.

Your fifty years ahead seem none too many?
20 Tell me how long I've got? God! For one year
To help myself to nothing more than air!
One Spring! Is one too good to spare, too long?
Spring wind would work its own way to my lung,
And grow me legs as quick as lilac-shoots.

25 My servant's lamed, but listen how he shouts!
When I'm lugged out, he'll still be good for that.
Here in this mummy-case, you know, I've thought
How well I might have swept his floors for ever.
I'd ask no nights off when the bustle's over,
30 Enjoying so the dirt. Who's prejudiced
Against a grimed hand when his own's quite dust,
Less live than specks that in the sun-shafts turn,
Less warm than dust that mixes with arms' tan?

I'd love to be a sweep, now, black as Town,
35   Yes, or a muckman. Must I be his load?

O Life, Life, let me breathe, – a dug-out rat!
Not worse than ours the lives rats lead –
Nosing along at night down some safe rut,
They find a shell-proof home before they rot.
40   Dead men may envy living mites in cheese,
Or good germs even. Microbes have their joys,
And subdivide, and never come to death.
Certainly flowers have the easiest time on earth.
'I shall be one with nature, herb, and stone,'
45   Shelley would tell me. Shelley would be stunned:
The dullest Tommy hugs that fancy now.
'Pushing up daisies' is their creed, you know.

To grain, then, go my fat, to buds my sap,
For all the usefulness there is in soap.
50   D'you think the Boche will ever stew man-soup?
Some day, no doubt, if . . .
                                    Friend, be very sure
I shall be better off with plants that share
More peaceably the meadow and the shower.
Soft rains will touch me, – as they could touch once,
55   And nothing but the sun shall make me ware.
Your guns may crash around me. I'll not hear;
Or, if I wince, I shall not know I wince.

Don't take my soul's poor comfort for your jest.
Soldiers may grow a soul when turned to fronds,
60   But here the thing's best left at home with friends.

My soul's a little grief, grappling your chest,
To climb your throat on sobs; easily chased
On other sighs and wiped by fresher winds.

Carry my crying spirit till it's weaned
65   To do without what blood remained these wounds.

Begun at Scarborough in December 1917 (WO, 248), and revised there in July 1918. On 3 December 1917 WO told SO: 'I finished an important poem this afternoon' (CL, 513), and three days later he wrote to SS: 'This "Wild with all Regrets" was begun & ended two days ago, at one gasp. If simplicity, if imaginativeness, if sympathy, if resonance of vowels, make poetry I have not succeeded. But if you say "Here is poetry," it will be so for me. What do you think of my Vowel-rime stunt in this, and "Vision"? Do you consider the hop from <u>Flea</u> to Soul too abrupt?' (CL, 514) At Ripon, in April 1918, 'Wild with all Regrets' was expanded into 'A Terre'.

    7 pennies: It was once customary to place coins on the eyelids of a corpse to keep them closed.

13–14 Cp. SS, 'Base Details', ll. 1–4:
> If I were fierce, and bald, and short of breath,
>   I'd live with scarlet Majors at the Base,
> And speed glum heroes up the line to death.
>   You'd see me with my puffy petulant face. . .

   19 Cp. A. E. Housman, 'Loveliest of trees, the cherry now', ll. 9–12:
> And since to look at things in bloom
> Fifty springs are little room,
> About the woodlands I will go
> To see the cherry hung with snow.

   30 dirt: Cp. No. 90, 'Inspection' (p. 95), l. 8: '"Well, blood is dirt," I said.'

   34 sweep: chimney-sweep.

   36 Cp. *King Lear*, v. iii. 307–8: 'Why should a dog, a horse, a rat, have life, / And thou no breath at all?'

   37 lives: Previous editors read 'existences', but see p. 354.

   44 The quotation is from Shelley, 'Adonais', xlii:
> He is made one with Nature: there is heard
> His voice in all her music, from the moan
> Of thunder, to the song of night's sweet bird;
> He is a presence to be felt and known
> In darkness and in light, from herb and stone,
> Spreading itself where'er that Power may move
> Which has withdrawn his being to its own . . .

   47 'Pushing up daisies': A common slang expression, meaning dead.

48–50 Cp. SS, 'The Tombstone-Maker', ll. 11–12: 'I told him with a sympathetic grin, / That Germans boil dead soldiers down for fat.'

54–5 Cp. No. 153, 'Futility' (p. 158), ll. 1–2: 'Move him into the sun – / Gently its touch awoke him once.'

   59 Cp. No. 139, 'Miners' (p. 135), l. 7: 'Frond-forests'.

MSS, p. 354

THE KIND GHOSTS

She sleeps on soft, last breaths; but no ghost looms
Out of the stillness of her palace wall,
Her wall of boys on boys and dooms on dooms.

She dreams of golden gardens and sweet glooms,
5 Not marvelling why her roses never fall
Nor what red mouths were torn to make their blooms.

The shades keep down which well might roam her hall.
Quiet their blood lies in her crimson rooms
And she is not afraid of their footfall.

10 They move not from her tapestries, their pall,
Nor pace her terraces, their hecatombs,
Lest aught she be disturbed, or grieved at all.

Revised – it may have been written earlier – at Scarborough on 30 July 1918, according to the dated MS, this may be the poem referred to in WO's letter to SO of 8 August 1918 (CL, 567).

1 She: Probably Britannia. DH notes that 'The word "Brittannia" (Owen's spelling was erratic) appears unexplained in a rough list of titles which he jotted down that summer; it seems likely to have been a draft title for this poem. Compare Swinburne's "Perinde ac Cadaver". While he was in France he acquired a copy of Swinburne's *Poems and Ballads*; it was probably the last book he read' (*Wilfred Owen* [Writers and Their Work, 1975], 35).

11 hecatombs: 'great public sacrifices' (*OED*). WO may have meant 'places of great public sacrifice'. Alternatively, he may have used the word, incorrectly, to mean 'tombs' or confused it with 'catacombs'.

MS, p. 357

170 SOLDIER'S DREAM

I dreamed kind Jesus fouled the big-gun gears;
And caused a permanent stoppage in all bolts;
And buckled with a smile Mausers and Colts;
And rusted every bayonet with His tears.

5 And there were no more bombs, of ours or Theirs,
Not even an old flint-lock, nor even a pikel.
But God was vexed, and gave all power to Michael;
And when I woke he'd seen to our repairs.

Begun at Craiglockhart in October 1917 and revised at Scarborough, probably that November and in July–August 1918. On 27 November 1917, WO wrote to SS: 'I trust you'll like the "Soldier's Dream" well enough to pass it on to the *Nation* or Cambridge? This was the last piece from Craiglockhart.' (CL, 512)

    3 Mausers and Colts: German and American brands of revolver.
    6 flint-lock: Old-fashioned gun with a flint in the hammer for striking a spark to ignite a charge of gunpowder.
    pikel: 'hay-fork or pitchfork' (*OED*), but perhaps here meant to suggest 'bayonet'.
    7 Michael: The Archangel commanding the heavenly armies.

MSS, p. 358

71   I am the ghost of Shadwell Stair.
        Along the wharves by the water-house,
        And through the cavernous slaughter-house,
    I am the shadow that walks there.

5   Yet I have flesh both firm and cool,
        And eyes tumultuous as the gems
        Of moons and lamps in the full Thames
    When dusk sails wavering down the Pool.

    Shuddering, a purple street-arc burns
10   Where I watch always. From the banks
        Dolorously the shipping clanks.
    And after me a strange tide turns.

    I walk till the stars of London wane,
        And dawn creeps up the Shadwell Stair.
15   But when the crowing sirens blare,
    I with another ghost am lain.

Drafted at Scarborough in January–February 1918, and revised there in July–August 1918, this poem, as DH notes, 'bears a marked similarity to Oscar Wilde's *Impression du Matin* and may have been a deliberate imitation. Shadwell Dock Stair is one of the many flights of steps leading from quay to water's edge along that part of the Thames known as the Pool of London.' (DH, 113)

    3 cavernous: Previous editors read 'dripping'.
    7 full: Previous editors read 'lapping'.
   12 Bäckman suggests (62) that the ghost is that of a prostitute after whom 'a strange tide [of men] turns'. The ghost may, indeed, have been intended to be that of the specific prostitute 'With lips of flame and heart of stone' in Wilde's poem.

MSS, p. 360

173 ELEGY IN APRIL AND SEPTEMBER
(jabbered among the trees)

1

Hush, thrush! Hush, missel-thrush, I listen . . .
I heard the flush of footsteps through loose leaves,
And a low whistle by the water's brim.

Still! daffodil! Nay, hail me not so gaily, –
5   Your gay gold lily daunts me and deceives,
Who follow gleams more golden and more slim.

Look, brook! O run and look, O run!
The vain reeds shook? – Yet search till grey sea heaves,
And I will stray among these fields for him.

10   Gaze, daisy! Stare through haze and glare,
And mark the hazardous stars all dawns and eves,
For my eye withers, and his star wanes dim.

2

Close, rose, and droop, heliotrope,
And shudder, hope! The shattering winter blows.
15   Drop, heliotrope, and close, rose . . .

Mourn, corn, and sigh, rye.
Men garner you, but youth's head lies forlorn.
Sigh, rye, and mourn, corn . . .

Brood, wood, and muse, yews,
20   The ways gods use we have not understood.
Muse, yews, and brood, wood . . .

Begun at Ripon in April–May 1918, this attempt at a pastoral elegy was continued in France the following September. On the back of one MS, WO has written 'Mat[t]hew Arnold' and beneath that a list beginning 'Thyr[s]is / Scholar Gipsy'; and it would seem that WO had Arnold's elegies in mind as models for his own. CDL prints only an earlier version of ll. 1–12.

> TITLE   The subject of this elegy – in one draft described as 'a Poet . . . reported killed' – has not been identified.
>
>   1 missel-thrush: WO wrote (and CDL reproduces his error) 'missen-thrush'.

MSS, p. 362

EXPOSURE

Our brains ache, in the merciless iced east winds that knive us . . .
Wearied we keep awake because the night is silent . . .
Low, drooping flares confuse our memory of the salient . . .
Worried by silence, sentries whisper, curious, nervous,
        But nothing happens.

Watching, we hear the mad gusts tugging on the wire,
Like twitching agonies of men among its brambles.
Northward, incessantly, the flickering gunnery rumbles,
Far off, like a dull rumour of some other war.
        What are we doing here?

The poignant misery of dawn begins to grow . . .
We only know war lasts, rain soaks, and clouds sag stormy.
Dawn massing in the east her melancholy army
Attacks once more in ranks on shivering ranks of grey,
        But nothing happens.

Sudden successive flights of bullets streak the silence.
Less deathly than the air that shudders black with snow,
With sidelong flowing flakes that flock, pause, and renew;
We watch them wandering up and down the wind's nonchalance,
        But nothing happens.

Pale flakes with fingering stealth come feeling for our faces –
We cringe in holes, back on forgotten dreams, and stare, snow-dazed,
Deep into grassier ditches. So we drowse, sun-dozed,
Littered with blossoms trickling where the blackbird fusses,
        – Is it that we are dying?

Slowly our ghosts drag home: glimpsing the sunk fires, glozed
With crusted dark-red jewels; crickets jingle there;
For hours the innocent mice rejoice: the house is theirs;
Shutters and doors, all closed: on us the doors are closed, –
        We turn back to our dying.

Since we believe not otherwise can kind fires burn;
Nor ever suns smile true on child, or field, or fruit.

> For God's invincible spring our love is made afraid;
> Therefore, not loath, we lie out here; therefore were born,
35   For love of God seems dying.
>
> Tonight, this frost will fasten on this mud and us,
> Shrivelling many hands, puckering foreheads crisp.
> The burying-party, picks and shovels in shaking grasp,
> Pause over half-known faces. All their eyes are ice,
40   But nothing happens.

Begun at Scarborough in December 1917, when one unfinished line was written at the top of the MS of No. 128, 'Cramped in that funnelled hole . . .' (p. 511); revised there in early 1918; and finished in France in September 1918, when its final draft was written on the same paper as that used for the second draft of No. 173, 'Elegy in April and September' (p. 184), which was composed in that month. WO appears to have dated the final draft of 'Exposure' 'Feb. 1916', but the '6' could be an imperfect '8' (wo, 246–8). EB suggested that WO may have intended to write 'Feb. 1917', since the poem stems from experiences described in a letter to SO dated 4 February 1917. (See DH, 'The Date of Wilfred Owen's "Exposure"', N&Q, n.s., xxiii, no. 7 [July 1976], 305–8.) On 22 April 1918, WO wrote to SO: 'to quote myself cynically "Nothing happens"' (CL, 548), which suggests that 'Exposure' was far enough advanced for her to be expected to recognize its refrain. It appears, under the title 'Nothing happens', in one of the lists of contents drawn up at Ripon between March and June 1918 (see Appendix B).

  1 An ironic echo of Keats, 'Ode to a Nightingale', ll. 1–2: 'My heart aches, and a drowsy numbness pains / My sense.'
  3 salient: The front line in places jutted into enemy territory, and at such 'salients' the fighting tended to be fiercest.
  9 Cp. Matthew 24:6: 'wars and rumours of wars'; also WO to ELG, 25 July 1915: 'You say you "hear of wars and rumours of wars". *Vous en êtes là seulement?* You hear Rumours? The rumours, over here, make the ears of the gunners bleed.' (CL, 349)
14 grey: The German troops wore grey uniforms and, like the dawn, came from the east.
22 Cp. No. 128, 'Cramped in that funnelled hole . . .' (p. 511).
23 drowse: See note on l. 1 above.
26 Cp. the song: 'Keep the home fires burning . . . Though your lads are far away they dream of home.'
     glozed: A conflation of 'glowing' and 'glazed'.

29 DH, in 'The Date of Wilfred Owen's "Exposure"', suggests a link with WO's postcard of 24 November 1917 to SO, in which he describes how he found himself at York in the small hours of the morning. The Station Hotel was full and 'the other hotels would not open to my knocking' (CL, 508).
33 God's invincible spring: Cp. No. 138, 'The Wrestlers' (p. 520): 'And all the ardour of the invincible spring'.
36 SS, EB, and CDL print 'His frost', an attractive but inaccurate reading.
39 All their eyes are ice: Cp. Yeats, 'The Happy Townland', l. 11: 'Queens, their eyes blue like the ice'.

MSS, p. 365

175 THE SENTRY

    We'd found an old Boche dug-out, and he knew,
    And gave us hell; for shell on frantic shell
    Lit full on top, but never quite burst through.
    Rain, guttering down in waterfalls of slime,
5   Kept slush waist-high and rising hour by hour,
    And choked the steps too thick with clay to climb.
    What murk of air remained stank old, and sour
    With fumes from whizz-bangs, and the smell of men
    Who'd lived there years, and left their curse in the den,
10 If not their corpses . . .
                     There we herded from the blast
    Of whizz-bangs; but one found our door at last, –
    Buffeting eyes and breath, snuffing the candles,
    And thud! flump! thud! down the steep steps came thumping
    And sploshing in the flood, deluging muck,
15 The sentry's body; then his rifle, handles
    Of old Boche bombs, and mud in ruck on ruck.
    We dredged it up, for dead, until he whined,
    'O sir – my eyes, – I'm blind, – I'm blind, – I'm blind.'
    Coaxing, I held a flame against his lids
20 And said if he could see the least blurred light
    He was not blind; in time they'd get all right.
    'I can't,' he sobbed. Eyeballs, huge-bulged like squids',
    Watch my dreams still, – yet I forgot him there
    In posting Next for duty, and sending a scout
25 To beg a stretcher somewhere, and flound'ring about
    To other posts under the shrieking air.

    Those other wretches, how they bled and spewed,
    And one who would have drowned himself for good, –
    I try not to remember these things now.
30 Let Dread hark back for one word only: how,
    Half-listening to that sentry's moans and jumps,
    And the wild chattering of his shivered teeth,
    Renewed most horribly whenever crumps
    Pummelled the roof and slogged the air beneath, –
35 Through the dense din, I say, we heard him shout
    'I see your lights!' – But ours had long gone out.

Begun at Craiglockhart between August and October 1917, continued at Scarborough in May 1918, and completed in France that September (WO, 274), this must be one of the 'few poems' that accompanied WO's letter of 22 September 1918 to SS (CL, 578). A year and a half before, on 16 January 1917, he had written to SO: 'In the Platoon on my left the sentries over the dug-out were blown to nothing. One of these poor fellows was my first servant whom I rejected. If I had kept him he would have lived, for servants don't do Sentry Duty. I kept my own sentries half way down the stairs during the more terrific bombardment. In spite of this one lad was blown down and, I am afraid, blinded.' (CL, 428). Previous editors follow an earlier MS.

    8 whizz-bangs: Small shells of such high velocity that the sound made in passing through the air is almost simultaneous with the explosion.

  22 Eyeballs: Cp. the other tormented eyes that stare from No. 144, 'Dulce et Decorum Est' (p. 140), l. 19, and No. 161, 'Greater Love' (p. 166), l. 6.

  25 flound'ring: Cp. letter of 16 January 1917 quoted above: 'I was mercifully helped to do my duty and crawl, wade, climb and flounder over No Man's Land to visit my other post' (CL, 427–8).

  28 one: Cp. letter quoted above: 'I nearly broke down and let myself drown in the water that was now slowly rising over my knees' (CL, 427).

MSS, p. 371

176 SMILE, SMILE, SMILE

Head to limp head, the sunk-eyed wounded scanned
Yesterday's *Mail*; the casualties (typed small)
And (large) Vast Booty from our Latest Haul.
Also, they read of Cheap Homes, not yet planned,
5 'For', said the paper, 'when this war is done
The men's first instincts will be making homes.
Meanwhile their foremost need is aerodromes,
It being certain war has but begun.
Peace would do wrong to our undying dead, –
10 The sons we offered might regret they died
If we got nothing lasting in their stead.
We must be solidly indemnified.
Though all be worthy Victory which all bought,
We rulers sitting in this ancient spot
15 Would wrong our very selves if we forgot
The greatest glory will be theirs who fought,
Who kept this nation in integrity.'
Nation? – The half-limbed readers did not chafe
But smiled at one another curiously
20 Like secret men who know their secret safe.
(This is the thing they know and never speak,
That England one by one had fled to France,
Not many elsewhere now, save under France.)
Pictures of these broad smiles appear each week,
25 And people in whose voice real feeling rings
Say: How they smile! They're happy now, poor things.

Written in France in mid- to late September 1918 (WO, 273–4). On 22 September, WO wrote to SS: 'Did you see what the Minister of Labour said in the *Mail* the other day? "The first instincts of the men <u>after the cessation of</u> hostilities will be to return home." And again –
"All classes <u>acknowledge</u> their indebtedness to the soldiers & sailors . . ."

  'About the same day, Clemenceau is reported by the *Times* as saying: "<u>All</u> are worthy . . . yet we should be untrue to ourselves if we forgot that the <u>greatest</u> glory will be to the splendid poilus, who, etc."

  'I began a Postscript to these Confessions, but hope you will already have lashed yourself, (lashed <u>yourself!</u>) into something . . .' (CL, 578) The *Times* of 19 September 1918 had reported the French premier as saying: 'All are worthy of victory, because they will know how to honour it. Yet, however, in the ancient spot where sit the fathers of the Republic we should be untrue to ourselves if we forgot that the greatest glory will be to those splendid *poilus* [French slang for 'common soldiers'] who will see confirmed by history the titles of nobility which they themselves have earned. At the present moment they ask for nothing more than to be allowed to complete the great work which will assure them of immortality. What do they want and what do you? To keep on fighting victoriously until the moment when the enemy will understand there is no possible negotiation between crime and right.'

TITLE Taken from one of the most popular British songs on the Western Front, which begins:
>   What's the use of worrying?
>   It never was worth while,
>   So, pack up your troubles in your old kit-bag
>   And smile, smile, smile.

MSS, p. 374

177 SPRING OFFENSIVE

Halted against the shade of a last hill
They fed, and eased of pack-loads, were at ease;
And leaning on the nearest chest or knees
Carelessly slept.
                But many there stood still
To face the stark blank sky beyond the ridge,
Knowing their feet had come to the end of the world.
Marvelling they stood, and watched the long grass swirled
By the May breeze, murmurous with wasp and midge;
And though the summer oozed into their veins
Like an injected drug for their bodies' pains,
Sharp on their souls hung the imminent ridge of grass,
Fearfully flashed the sky's mysterious glass.

Hour after hour they ponder the warm field
And the far valley behind, where buttercups
Had blessed with gold their slow boots coming up;
When even the little brambles would not yield
But clutched and clung to them like sorrowing arms.
They breathe like trees unstirred.

Till like a cold gust thrills the little word
At which each body and its soul begird
And tighten them for battle. No alarms
Of bugles, no high flags, no clamorous haste, –
Only a lift and flare of eyes that faced
The sun, like a friend with whom their love is done.
O larger shone that smile against the sun, –
Mightier than his whose bounty these have spurned.

So, soon they topped the hill, and raced together
Over an open stretch of herb and heather
Exposed. And instantly the whole sky burned
With fury against them; earth set sudden cups
In thousands for their blood; and the green slope
Chasmed and deepened sheer to infinite space.

Of them who running on that last high place

     Breasted the surf of bullets, or went up
35 On the hot blast and fury of hell's upsurge,
     Or plunged and fell away past this world's verge,
     Some say God caught them even before they fell.

     But what say such as from existence' brink
     Ventured but drave too swift to sink,
40 The few who rushed in the body to enter hell,
     And there out-fiending all its fiends and flames
     With superhuman inhumanities,
     Long-famous glories, immemorial shames –
     And crawling slowly back, have by degrees
45 Regained cool peaceful air in wonder –
     Why speak not they of comrades that went under?

Begun probably at Scarborough in July 1918, this poem was revised in France in mid- to late September (WO, 274–6). A fair copy of ll. 1–17 was sent with WO's letter of 22 September 1918 to SS. An accompanying note asked: 'Is this worth going on with? I don't want to write anything to which a soldier would say No Compris!' (CU) There is no evidence that SS replied. The poem draws on WO's experience of the Allies' 'spring offensive' in April 1917 (WO, 178–82), and its MSS show that it was never finally revised.

    2–3 Previous editors read: 'They fed, and lying easy, were at ease / And, finding comfortable chests and knees,'
    11 ridge: Previous editors read 'line'.
  14–15 buttercups: Previous editors read 'the buttercup'. WO had coined the image of l. 15 in 1907, returning through the fields to Shrewsbury after Evensong in Uffington Church. HO remembered: 'Wilfred gently pressed my arm for silence – hesitated a moment and then called quietly back, "Harold's boots are blessed with gold"' (JFO, I. 176). The image subsequently appeared in No. 65, 'A Palinode' (p. 77), ll. 17–20:
        But if the sovereign sun I might behold
        With condescension coming down benign,
        And blessing all the field and air with gold,
        Then the contentment of the world was mine.
      Cp. also Keats, 'To Autumn', ll. 2–4:
        Close bosom-friend of the maturing sun;
        Conspiring with him how to load and bless
        With fruit the vines that round the thatch-eaves run. . . .
    16 When: Previous editors read 'Where'.
    17 arms: Previous editors read 'hands'.

18 The MS reads: 'All they strange day they breathe like trees unstirred', and one must suppose that WO intended to find alternatives for the cancelled words.

23–5 Cp. WO to CO, 14 May 1917: 'And his face shone with the brightness of the sun' (CL, 459).

29–31 Cp. Henri Barbusse, *Under Fire* (1917), 244: 'Abruptly, across all the width of the opposite slope, lurid flames burst forth that strike the air with terrible detonations. In line from left to right fires emerge from the sky and explosions from the ground.'

30 DH notes 'The word *cups* suggests not only shell-holes but also *buttercup[s]* (l. 14) and chalices, cups which are used in the Mass to contain the wine which is both a blessing (cf. *blessed with gold*) and sacrificial blood. Having refused the offered blessing of communion with the natural order, the men have become victims sacrificed to an outraged Nature.' (DH, 135) Dr Ellen Sarot has detected an echo of Genesis 4: 10–11: 'The voice of thy brother's blood crieth unto me from the ground. And now art thou cursed from the earth, which hath opened her mouth to receive thy brother's blood from thy hand. . . .'

33 last high place: 'another reference to sacrifice – hilltop sacrificial altars were known in ancient times as "high places"' (DH, 135).

34 Previous editors read: 'Leapt to swift unseen bullets, or went up'. EB misread 'surf' as 'swift'. Of the variant, and mainly cancelled, forms of this line (see transcript on p. 378), I prefer one first proposed by Welland.

MSS, p. 376

821.912
OWEN, WILFRED
WILFRED OWEN, THE COMPLETE
POEMS AND FRAGMENTS VOL. II

1

RECEIVED APR 1 3 1984 £5.00

NBAB 4/7/97
To ~~Montruk~~ - due ~~4/21/97~~

0300183504

RECEIVED APR 1 3 1984 65.00

821.912
OWEN, WILFRED
WILFRED OWEN, THE COMPLETE
   POEMS AND FRAGMENT VOL. I

1

South Huntington Public Library
Huntington Station, New York
11746

005

RECEIVED APR 1 3 1984   65.00

821.912
OWEN, WILFRED
WILFRED OWEN, THE COMPLETE
  POEMS AND FRAGMENT VOL. I

1

South Huntington Public Library
Huntington Station, New York
11746

RECEIVED APR 1 3 1984 65.00

821.912
OWEN, WILFRED
WILFRED OWEN, THE COMPLETE
POEMS AND FRAGMENT VOL. I

South Huntington Public Library
Huntington Station, New York
11746

ATHLETICS